The Deleuze Connections

John Rajchman

The Deleuze Connections

The MIT Press   Cambridge, Massachusetts   London, England

This book was set in Garamond 3, Bembo, and Meta by Graphic Composition, Inc., Athens, Georgia, and was printed and bound in the United States of America.

Library of Congress Cataloging-in-Publication Data

Rajchman, John.

The Deleuze connections / John Rajchman.

p. cm.

Includes bibliographical references.

ISBN 0-262-18205-X (hc. : alk. paper) — ISBN 0-262-68120-X (pbk. : alk. paper)

1. Deleuze, Gilles. I. Title.

B2430.D454 R34 2000

194—dc21   00-032917

Contents

Works by Deleuze

AO   *L'anti-oedipe* (Minuit, 1972) (with Félix Guattari)

B   *Le Bergsonisme* (Presses universitaires de France, 1966)

C1   *Cinéma 1—l'image-mouvement* (Minuit, 1983)

C2   *Cinéma 2—l'image-temps* (Minuit, 1985)

CC   *Critique et clinique* (Minuit, 1993)

D   *Dialogues* (Flammarion, 1977), trans (Columbia 1987) (with Claire Parnet)

DR   *Différence et répétition* (Presses universitaires de France, 1969)

E   *Empirisme et subjectivité* (Presses universitaires de France, 1953)

FB   *Francis Bacon: logique de la sensation* (Différence, 1981)

F   *Foucault* (Minuit, 1986)

K   *Kafka: pour une littérature mineure* (Minuit, 1975) (with Félix Guattari)

LS   *Logique du sens* (Minuit, 1969)

MP   *Mille Plateaux* (Minuit, 1980) (with Félix Guattari)

MPR   *Marcel Proust et les signes* (Presses universitaires de France, 1964, 1970)

N   *Nietzsche et la philosophie* (Presses universitaires de France, 1962)

PI   *Pure Immanence: Essays on a Life* (Zone, 2001)

PK   *La philosophie de Kant* (Presses universitaires de France, 1963)

PLI   *Le pli: Leibniz et le baroque* (Minuit, 1988)

PP   *Pourparlers* (Minuit, 1990)

PSM   *Présentation de Sacher-Masoch* (Minuit, 1967)

QP   *Qu'est-ce que la philosophie* (Minuit, 1991) (with Félix Guattari)

SP   *Spinoza et le probléme de l'expression* (Minuit, 1968)

SPP   *Spinoza—philosophie pratique* (Minuit, 1981)

The Deleuze Connections

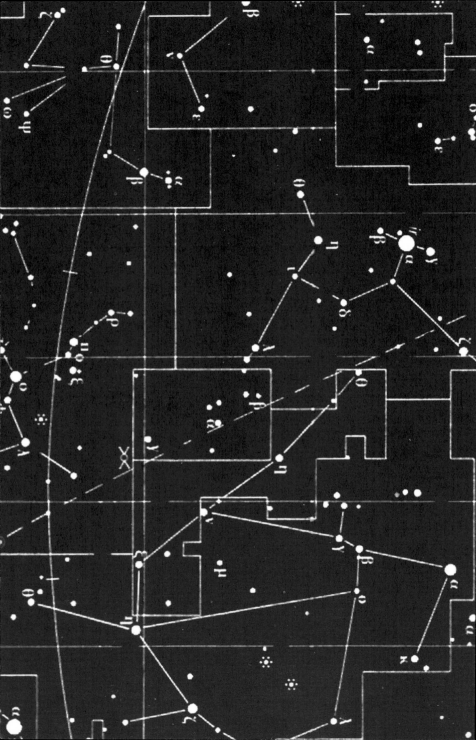

I: *Connections*

This book is a map of Deleuze's philosophy, made from a particular perspective. It asks: can one extract from Deleuze a style of thought, a way of doing philosophy, which one might carry on today in much altered circumstances, artistic and political, from those that divided up philosophy after the Second World War through which Deleuze himself navigated?

This book is a map, but not a program, a plan, a project. It is made up of many connections, intended to suggest others—connections of a peculiar sort. For of course Deleuze's philosophy is about connections; in some sense, it *is* an art of multiple things held together by "disjunctive syntheses," by logical conjunctions prior and irreducible to predication or identification. Such indeed is its principle of selection or affirmation: *"Only retain . . . what augments the number of connections."*[1] The principle is at work in Deleuze's own style of writing by "series" or "plateaus," which discourages any unified plan of organization or development in favor of an unlimited plane in which one is always passing from one singular point to another, then connecting it to yet something else. The connections that make up the map of this book try to respect this logic; and in this way it approaches the larger question of how to do philosophy—of new ways of "connecting" philosophy, and connecting *with* philosophy. In an earlier book called *Constructions,* I sought to create a zone of new connections between philosophy and architecture, art, and urbanism. But what kind of thinking was thus put into practice; how might it lead to the formulation of new problems, the invention of new concepts; and what are its social and political implications? This book, this map, tries to further elaborate and enlarge those questions.

This book is thus a map meant for those who want to take up or take on Deleuze philosophically as well as those engaged in what Deleuze called the "nonphilosophical understanding of philosophy." It is unlikely to work for those minds that are already settled, already classified, armed with the now increasingly useless maps of "postmodernism," "poststructuralism," or the old continental-analytic divide. It is for those whose minds or identities are not already made up, who are willing to embark on the sort of voyage where one throws out one's hermeneutic compass and leaves one's discourse behind, the sort of voyage for which Deleuze adopted the Proustian motto: the true dreamer is the one who goes out to try to verify something. In other words, it is not a map in which to locate or recognize oneself in a predetermined plane with fixed coordinates. It appeals to another kind of philosophical "orientation." It tries to work with zones that are precisely not completely determined or localizing, where things may go off in unforeseen directions or work in unregulated ways—with a "sense" of logic rather different from the traditional philosophical one. Deleuze tries to show that in contrast to the traditional logical sense, there exist such zones of indetermination, secretly accompanying most forms of organization, and that thinking has a peculiar relation to them. For to think is to experiment and not, in the first place, to judge. Deleuze's way out of the great Kantian philosophical figure of the judge at the tribunal of reason was to depart from the presumption of a "common sense," logical, moral, aesthetic, that underlies Kant's philosophy, but which Kant himself, perhaps, in a last moment when he dreamt of an unregulation of the very faculties whose limits he had worked so hard to establish, suggested a way to undo. A map of connections as distinct from localizing points is thus a map for a "we" not given through a presumption of common sense—for a people that is missing, not already there, unable to find its place in the distinction between public and private, and so much come from "the outside." It is a map meant for those who want to *do* something with respect to new uncommon forces, which we don't quite yet grasp, who have a certain taste for the unknown, for what is not already determined by history or society. For it is through such experimentation that we escape from the nostalgia of "antiquarian" history as well as "progressivism" that already knows what is to come.

Several principles of connection follow.

1. Connection requires a style of thought that might be called "empiricist" or "pragmatist." It puts experimentation before ontology, "And" before "Is." The principle of such a pragmatism is posed in the first sentences of *A Thousand Plateaus,* where Deleuze and Guattari declare that multiplicity, more than a matter of logic, is something one must make or do, and learn by making or doing—*le multiple, il faut le faire.*[2] We must always *make* connections, since they are not already given. Such is the empiricist principle Deleuze finds already in Hume's associations, understood as "relations external to their terms," and the way they eventually lead to a jurisprudence of "conventions" prior to the violence of social "partialities." Hume thus anticipates what is to come after Kant and the impasse of the search for "transcendental conditions of possibility." He anticipates the type of conceptual experimenter who crosses the bounds or frames of common sense and forges relations and connections prior to it. What is supposed by such experimental crossing of borders is not so much hope as a kind of trust or confidence—a belief-in-the-world. To connect is to then to work with other possibilities, not already given; but utopian is not the best word

for them, so much is it still part of the dream of organization, development, or else of some sort of mystical messianism of a "nonidentity" called upon to interrupt continuities. Deleuze tries to rethink the whole logic of possibility and its relations with fiction and reality, and so rediscovers in our selves and our world a Humean sense of an artifice in which we come to believe. It is not so much a matter of being optimistic or pessimistic as of being realistic about the new forces not already contained in our projects and programs and the ways of thinking that accompany them. In other words, to make connections one needs not knowledge, certainty, or even ontology, but rather a trust that something may come out, though one is not yet completely sure what. Hume substituted for Cartesian certainty a probability of belief, but Deleuze pushes the question of belief into that zone of an "improbable chance" that no throw of the dice can abolish.

2. We must thus *make* connections, ever more connections. But this pragmatism—this And—is not an instrumentalism, and it supposes another sense of machine. It is not determined by given outcomes, not based in predictive expertise. On the contrary, its motto is "not to predict, but to remain attentive to the unknown knocking at the door."[3] The "machines" Kafka set up are like this: without nostalgia, they point to the "diabolical forces" of what is yet to come, for "strictly speaking, what makes a machine are connections, all the connections that guide the dismantling."[4] More generally, talk of machines and of "phylums" of machine in Deleuze (e.g., the mechanical and informational phylums) follows this principle. Instruments are always part of larger sorts of "arrangements" or "assemblages" that then allow for "machinic connections" of another, noninstrumentalized, even improbable, sort, which may then be taken up by thought. Thinking is

understood through the uses to which it gives rise, the connections it opens. But for that, it needs the sobriety of a certain realism. Often it is a matter of making visible problems for which there exists no program, no plan, no "collective agency," problems that therefore call for new groups, not yet defined, who must invent themselves in the process in accordance with affects or passions of thinking prior to common cognition and its codes.

3. Making connections involves a logic of a peculiar sort. Outside established identities, divisions, and determinations, logical and syntactical as well as pragmatic, it has often been assumed that there is only chaos, anarchy, undifferentiation, or "absurdity." Deleuze tries to expose this illusion, and to advance a conception that allows for a layer of sense prior to code, even a structuralist one, as well as to fixed subjective positions and relations. His own logic of converging and diverging series tries to work with such a sense. In developing it, he encounters the great attempts in contemporary philosophy to move beyond the transcendental logic of Husserl or the symbolic logic of Frege and find a looser kind of sense, closer to life itself—the "grammar" that Wittgenstein associated with forms of life, or the kind of embodied existence or "flesh" that Merleau-Ponty posited prior to the objectivities of the "natural attitude."[5] Thus Deleuze declares that Fregean logic is necessarily reductive of the kind of complications and ramifications required for thought, while Merleau-Ponty's notion of the flesh still harbors a strange piety, tied up with a dream of an originary experience or Urdoxa. *His* "abstract machines" are built from many local connections, each with their "concrete rules," not globally set; thus they are not Turing machines, indifferent to materials, even ones armed with recursive functions. On the other hand, the "being of sensation"

that one extracts from common perceptions and personalized affects, or from the space of representation and the reidentification of objects, leads not to an intersubjective orientation in the world, but rather to a mad zone of indetermination and experimentation from which new connections may emerge. In Deleuze's logic, a kind of uncoded "diagram" replaces the "schematism" that tries to unite sensation and cognition; and through it, one attains a plan "not in the sense of mental design, a project, a program," but rather "in the geometric sense: a section, an intersection, a diagram."[6] Deleuze wants to make this kind of plan essential to our thinking. Thus, starting with Plato, he tries to stage a dramatic reorientation of the very *agon* of philosophy, and of the nature of the friends or *philoi* who engage in it. Philosophy acquires a new adversary: its aim is to combat the "stupidity" that consists in that sad state of ourselves and the world in which we can't, or don't, or don't want to, any longer make connections. Around this new contest and game the "friends of thought" would gather again.

4. Classical philosophy was directed against superstition and error; and no doubt there is still need for such an orientation of thought. But philosophy would confront other problems, discover other orientations. In the nineteenth century Deleuze thinks there emerges a new problem—the stupidity of which Foucault would say that opposite is not a cognitive intelligence but the perilous activity of thought itself.[7] Flaubert helps introduce the problem into literature: Bouvard and Pecuchet expose the stupidity of the encyclopedia whose image still haunted Hegel. More generally Deleuze finds a sort of parallel movement in modern works of arts: the great struggle to free sensation or *aisthesis* from clichés or mere "probabilities" and discover the

mad change of singularities. For, as Deleuze puts it in his analysis of postwar cinema, we live in a civilization not of the image, but of clichés, in which the whole question is precisely to extract a genuine image.[8] To break out of stupidity, a certain violence is required—a shock, an "alienation-effect," or else the sort of the "cruelty" Deleuze admired in Artaud's attempt to extract the body from organistic representation. In each case one must devise new procedures to free affect from personal feeling, percept from common perception, and in a phrase Deleuze takes from Proust, to create a foreign language in our language, to be spoken by a people that does not yet exist. When as in Nietzsche, or in another way in Foucault, the problem of such stupidity is introduced into philosophy, we find these features: thinking is inseparable from a violence that problematizes or shakes up *doxa* and gives something new to be thought; and to conceive of it one needs the violence or "strangeness" of what can't yet be said in the dominant or "common" language. Thus philosophy always uses words in ways not comprehended or fixed by their antecedents; and it starts not in a natural or God-given "desire for truth," but in the reorientation that arises when it is thus disturbed. Deleuze therefore opposes the "illusion of communication" already found in the intersubjectivity and Urdoxa Husserl sought, which would pacify the violence of thought and eliminate the element of "stupidity" once and for all.

5. In *Difference and Repetition,* the stupidities Deleuze considers are often the familiar mechanistic or industrial ones, against which would be ranged the labyrinthine complications of the nouveau roman or the "simulacral" deviations in Warhol's series. But twenty years later, in his study of cinema, the problem of such "mechanical automatisms" has been replaced by that of the new

forces of information-machines and the questions they introduce—for example, the question of how information and interaction are "framed" so as to allow for common sense.[9] Thus there
arises a new enemy of thought, more insolent and self-assured
than those of the last century—a *communicational stupidity,* to
which corresponds a new form of power which Deleuze proposed
to call "control." "We are at the start of something new," he wrote
in 1990.[10] We need to better diagnose the new forces, biotechnological as well as digital, and the larger social and economic
processes from which they are inseparable; there might then arise
a new *Kunstwollen,* a new "becoming-art" to deliver us from our
communicational stupidities, our informational "automatisms."

Today Deleuze's language of connection, rhizome, network
may well sound like talk of neural nets or internets, but one must
proceed with caution. For he in fact rejected the computer model
of the mind. He wanted to allow for those margins of sense given
by affect and percept which, though irreducible to "cognition,"
are nevertheless required for thought. Starting in his study of cinema, he develops an original view of a brain that no longer functions by plan or program—an uncertain, probabilistic brain he
found suggested in microbiological research. In postwar film he
sees a "lived brain," which works by "irrational" connections,
prior to mental states; and more generally, following Bergson, he
proposes that for the reductive materialism of such states we substitute an expressive materialism in which, beyond the "objec-
tivized" brain, art as well as philosophy might create multiple
new paths or synapses, not already given—new connections.

6. In social terms, connections are not social interactions between already constituted subjects; they are at once "smaller"
and "larger" than individuals and suppose a kind of sociality

not based on the mechanisms of collective recognition or identification. Deleuze's basic principle is that society is always *en fuite* (leaking, fleeing) and may be understood in terms of the manner in which it deals with its *fuites* (leaks, lines of flight). It says there is no determination of ourselves that does not at the same time create zones of indetermination—indetermination with respect to our individualizations as persons, sexes or genders, classes or strata, even as members of the human species. Such zones are then the ones from which original "connections" may come; they are the ones that allow for the encounters, which, starting with Gabriel Tarde, microsociology began to explore.[11] But here "micro" doesn't mean "individual"; on the contrary, it supposes a "mass" that is not yet "individualized"; and the question it raises is not about individuals and contracts, but about singularities and the space and time in which they can coexist.[12] Minority is thus not the same as ethnic identity. On the contrary, it is a matter of this "people to come" to which Kafka appealed when he wrote to Max Brod that he couldn't write in German, in Czech, or in Yiddish, and yet could not *not* write. Deleuze does not hesitate to draw this political consequence, elaborated in his account of third world and minority cinema: "we no longer dispose of an image of the proletariat of which it would suffice to become self-conscious."[13] Thus he asks what an analysis of capitalism would look like if, instead of being based on a simple dialectic of already constituted classes, it introduced the question of minorities and zones of indetermination, and so looked for those larger processes that "deterritorialized" or "uncoded" our relations to ourselves and one another. He tries to imagine what an ethos, and therefore an ethic, might be that put deterritorialization first, starting with our very conception of ourselves and "the other."

7. In the history of philosophy, the concepts Deleuze finds for the zone in which connections can be made are Substance in Spinoza and Life in Nietzsche; and in the 1960s he developed ingenious interpretations of each philosopher to show this, thus linking the two together in a new way. In Spinoza, he finds a "plan of composition" prior to a "plan of organization or development," and in Nietzsche, a light or deterritorialized Earth, prior to identities, given through a nomadic relation to borders or boundaries. Together they offer the principle of affirmation and selection, which says: "keep only what increases connections." For to affirm is not to assert or assume, but to lighten, to unground, to release the fresh air of other possibilities, to combat stupidity and cliché. From the start Deleuze was a philosopher not of negation but of affirmation—not of mourning and absence, not of sad, tired ironies, but of humor and life. Together with Guattari he elaborated a conception of desire itself no longer based in sacrifice or privation, working instead as a kind of great connection-machine; and against the melancholy model of the blank page or empty canvas, he proposed a view in which the page or canvas is always covered over with too many clichés, too many probabilities, which must be cleared away in order to find something vital, something new. He tried to recast the problem of novelty and originality accordingly, not as transgression or mystical "interruption" but rather as a great art of connection and experimentation. To Oedipus and his tragic fate he opposed Hamlet and the complex "time of the city" that can go out of joint; and instead of Antigone and the Law he was drawn to Ariadne, figure of lightness and affirmation. For to connect is to affirm, and to affirm, to connect.

2: *Experiment*

1

Deleuze's first book was about Hume. Published in 1953 when he was 26, it was an attempt to rethink empiricism. The secret of empiricism, he thought, belongs to philosophy itself and not simply to its views on knowledge or science; and it is in Hume that this secret emerges. With Hume, empiricism discovers new powers, even a new logic, irreducible to the textbook definition that everything derives from experience or that there exist no innate or a priori ideas.[1] There is a new image of the relation of thought to experience—a new sense of the illusions against which philosophy is directed and of the nature of the drama of those who enter into it. In unraveling this secret, and so reformulating the sense or the problem of empiricism, Deleuze saw this early study of Hume as a work of philosophy and not simply of the history of philosophy. Gradually he would make this problem and this sense his own.

For the young Deleuze, then, Hume's shift from a world of Cartesian certainty to one of probable belief belonged to a larger change in the very image of what it is to do philosophy, and the sorts of relations it supposes with other activities, which, in turn, was to have a long history. A great adversary in this history was Kant, who, in response to Hume, turned philosophy into a court of judgment concerned with the conditions of possibility of true judgments. In place of this image, Deleuze would propose a philosophy of experimentation. Starting with Deleuze's essays in the 1950s, on the conception of difference in Bergson, he sought a "superior empiricism" that would survive Kant and assume new forms in post-Kantian thought. The problem was to overcome a basic difficulty Kant had introduced into philosophy: that the transcendental conditions of thought or the determination of the "I think" were in fact always modeled on the "empirical" domains they were supposed to found. The solution to such "transcendental-empirical doubling" was to invent an experimentalism, which, instead of asking for conditions of possible experience, would look for the conditions under which something new, as yet unthought, arises. Bergson would introduce a conception of such "difference" into the formation of subject and object, finding in the words of William James an empiricism "not of things made but of things in the making."[2] Philosophy would then cease to be correction of error, and turn to what in experience, or in life, is prior to subjects and the objects to which they refer. The "problem of subjectivity" Deleuze finds in his early study of Hume is that the self is not given, but formed through habit from an indeterminate world, and is itself a strange kind of "fiction" difficult to dissipate, since it is precisely the fiction of ourselves and our world.[3] This "artifice," the determination of self, would then already be deepened in Kant, the indetermination in the formation of the "I think" would find an original relation to temporality, which Bergson or James would later try to free from the idea of extension or of "the block universe." One arrives in this way at the possibility of constructions in experience prior to subjects and objects—what Deleuze would come to call a "plane of immanence." Sartre would approach it in formulating a "transcendence of the ego"; Foucault would rediscover it in his attempt to work out an impersonality or anonymity of discourse, prior to the specification of subjects and referents, as condition of "events" of thought. In each case Deleuze would see a "superior empiricism" prior to any transcendental subjectivity or intersubjectivity—a sort of philosophical experimentalism that would suppose a "pure immanence," with no first or transcendental elements, or which would not be immanent *to* anything prior, either subjective or objective.[4]

In this manner the secret of empiricism would become a secret of a whole philosophy—a singular view of how and what it means to do conduct philosophy. There is nothing quite like it in any language. It doesn't easily fit in our accustomed divisions and ways of doing philosophy, and yet, in the much-altered geographies and climates today, it might yet attract new connections, somewhat different from those offered by the postwar French philosophy from which it emerged, and so acquire new uses, new possibilities, a new life.

2 We are accustomed to enclosing empiricism within the "analysis" of Russell's logic, and opposing to it the historicism or metaphysics of the Continent, perhaps counting the holism of Quine as a correction of its "protocol" in Viennese philosophy. But Deleuze takes Hume in another direction, finding associations not simply with themes and problems in the history of philosophy, but also with those of Lewis Carroll, Alfred Hitchcock, or Herman Melville. He would see it in Stoicism, and in its sense of surfaces freed from heights and depths, he would anticipate a spatiality he would later see in the painting of Francis Bacon—only Englishmen and Stoics have really understood the event, he would declare with distinctive humor. But at the same time his "empiricism" would distinguish Deleuze among his French contemporaries. Empiricism was Deleuze's way out of phenomenology, Foucault would say;[5] but it would also be part of the "pragmatics" he would oppose to the "postulates of linguistics" in Chomsky or in Saussurian structuralism.[6] Deleuze would try to relieve the philosophy of his French contemporaries of the temptation to reinstall transcendence—in particular, in the form of a peculiar mysticism of the Invisible or the Absent, or the Unrepresentable and its supposed Law, opposing to it an experimentalism of what, in reference to Blanchot, Foucault had called "the outside." "Too pious, still too pious," Deleuze kept saying of such transcendence of the Law or of the "flesh of the world"—still too much of the figure of the priest from which Nietzsche had tried to free philosophy, too much of the "politico-theological" arrangement from which Spinoza had found a way out, not enough of the "empiricist conversion" to be found in American pragmatism, which substitutes experimentation for salvation.[7]

It might then seem that there are affinities between Deleuze's work and Feyerabend's "empiricism" of the proliferation of incommensurable or nonunified programs in science; and in relation to Foucault, Deleuze spoke of a pluralism that lies in the way reason is always "bifurcating," ever finding new styles and problems.[8] But when he explains to his English readers that "I have always felt that I am an empiricist, that is a pluralist," it is rather by reference to Whitehead's critique of abstractions and of "specious concreteness."[9] His affinities lie more explicitly with the "radical empiricism" of James, and with the attempt to push the question of belief beyond the "warrant" of assertability or agreements. That is one way he differs from Richard Rorty, who in fact got his start by abandoning his youthful enthusiasm for Whitehead in favor of a kind of evolving cultural "conversation."[10] In Hume's *Dialogues on Natural Religion* Deleuze already finds a style of dialogue or conversation given not so much by agreement as by a humor that takes us beyond the linguistic practices of agreement and solidarity within which Rorty's own pragmatism or empiricism would be remain mired.[11]

Empiricism is about relations—the sort of relations Hume took to make up "human nature." But those relations need not be founded in agreement or common sense. Russell showed relations are "external to the terms," but one must push this idea beyond the predicate logic within which Russell still worked to that element in "sense" which is precisely prior to agreements and propositions. An originality of Deleuze is to free empiricism from the assumptions of a "common sense," and to say that the consistency or coherence of concepts in philosophy owes its existence to the problems introduced by an "outside" that comes before things "settle" into agreements and persists within them. He pushes the experience or experimentalism of thought into a zone before the establishment of a stable, intersubjective "we," and makes it a matter not of recognizing ourselves or the things in our world, but rather of encounter with what we can't yet "determine"—to what we can't yet describe or agree upon, since we don't yet even have the words. Thus we must thus resist the Kantian attempt to turn Hume's "relations" into transcendental conditions of the I Think; rather we should see them in "pragmatic" or "wordly" terms, as already with the notion of convention in Hume. Only then do we see that the full force of Hume's formulation of the "problem of subjectivity" lies in his view of the passions and the artifice in their expression, which allows us to go beyond our social identities and see society as experiment rather than contract. The problem of "experience" or "experiment" in philosophy in short becomes one of forging conceptual relations not already given in constructions whose elements fit together not like pieces of a puzzle but rather like disparate stones brought together temporally in an as yet uncemented wall.[12]

3

Deleuze's empiricism is then shown in his style of constructing his philosophy, and the manner in which he expounds its concepts or presents its ideas.

"I never broke with a sort of empiricism that proceeds to a direct exposition of concepts," he declares: perhaps that is what made him the most "naif," the most "innocent" among his contemporaries concerned with similar themes, the one who least had a bad conscience about doing philosophy.[13] Deleuze found the overdramatic worries about the "end of philosophy" to be so much "tiresome blather."[14] In the face of such melancholy themes, he tried to practice philosophy as an *art brut*—a sort of "outsiders' art," with its "own raw materials that permit it to enter into external relations . . . with other disciplines."[15] He envisaged philosophy as a sort of detective story with concepts for characters, intervening to resolve local problems, then themselves changing as fresh questions emerge and new dramas take shape.

We might then imagine Deleuze's philosophy as built up in a way such as this: there are different conceptual "bits," each initially introduced in relation to a particular problem, then reintroduced into new contexts, seen from new perspectives. The coherence among the various bits shifts from one work to the next as new concepts are added, fresh problems addressed; it is not given by "logical consistency" among propositions, but rather by the "series" or "plateaus" into which the conceptual pieces enter or settle along the web of their interrelations. There are new "encounters" with problems that arise in the arts or sciences, or with events that "problematize" the ways politics is conducted or society held together, introducing new questions that call for a rethinking or reinvention. The bits thus don't work together like parts in a well-formed organism or a purposeful mechanism or a well-formed narrative—the whole is not given, and things are always starting up again in the middle, falling together in another looser way. As one thus passes from one zone or "plateau" to another and back again, one thus has nothing of the sense of a well-planned itinerary; on the contrary, one is taken on a sort of conceptual trip for which there preexists no map—a voyage for which one must leave one's usual discourse behind and never be quite be sure where one will land.

Among the concepts, problems, and dramas that make up the various "bits" in this construction, some are derived from a fresh look at the work of previous philosophers, taking up their problems from a new angle. For already in his youthful study of Hume, Deleuze thought one can do philosophy "off the backs" of predecessors, casting basic problems and concepts in a new light. For his own case, this would particularly be true for the concept and problem of difference he found in Bergson, or through which he tried to rethink Bergsonism. This is true of the "problem of empiricism" itself. Extracted through Hume from the textbook definition, the problem would enter into the work of other philosophers; it would be found in one way in Bergson, another in Sartre, yet another in Foucault. Thus Deleuze finds an "empiricism" in Nietzsche and an "experimentalism" in Spinoza, which in turn discover an "underground" lineage with Lucretius; and a new problem, a new "detective story" emerges—the problem of how to "believe in the world."

But this incessant passage from one bit to another, this "nomadic" roaming about, is in itself a kind of "empiricism." It is a way of departing from the compartmentalization of knowledge, yet without recourse to an organic unity (Romantic nostalgia for its loss), and in a manner at odds with the idea of the university as internalization of a higher Republic, as in the tradition of the public professor that goes from Kant to Hegel or Habermas. In Deleuze's empiricism, philosophy always starts in an encounter with something outside the Academy, and the mutual recognition of transcendental selves it would embody or guard as judge and watchman. He thought Sartre played this role for his generation, pointing to something outside the "probabilities of the Sorbonne." But it was Nietzsche, in his break with Wagner and his abandonment of his professorship in Basel, who would formulate the relevant distinction, when he contrasted "private thinker" with "public professor"; and Nietzsche himself would become at once empiricist and nomadic in the manner of the wandering Zarathustra when he declares "I came to my truth in many ways, by many ways . . . for *the* way does not exist." Similarly, Spinoza would turn down the offer of a public professorship, preferring to work with his circle of friends and students, in accordance with a view of the nature or function of philosophy that might be contrasted with that of Hobbes, public professor;[16] and even the appeal to an endless community of inquirers with an experimental spirit advanced before the Metaphysical Club by the solitary cantankerous Peirce might be read along such lines rather than as an anticipation of a reliance on the agreements of social-scientific expertise. Deleuze's empiricism in short is against Schools and their methods, and he neither belonged to nor founded one. He wanted to free the "pedagogy of the concept" from the encyclopedic image that haunted Hegel and make it more akin to Godard's "pedagogy of the image," and then to defend it against a new informational-communicational training of thought and image he feared was replacing the older encyclopedic ideal. Directed against Schools and avant-gardes, Deleuze's empiricism nevertheless calls for a rigor or logic of another kind, even if it is that of a method that orders in advance, and involves a kind of selection. It is not at all a matter of anything goes.

4 Deleuze's multiple accretion through encounter, his nonmethodical rigor of the intuitions of problems and concepts, is shown in turn by the manner in which his philosophy grows and acquires a coherence of its own. Growth is not linear; it is not "developmental" (with early, middle, and later phases); it doesn't proceed by successive crises of the sort Deleuze found in Foucault (where "the logic of the work" lay in crises it went);[17] there is no great dramatic turning point, as in Wittgentsein or Heidegger, where one style of philosophy is abandoned in favor of another, nor even the kind of voyage to innocence Deleuze found in the phases of Nietzsche's philosophy.[18] As it grows, his philosophy doesn't become more "mature," but rather more complex and multiple in its implications and its reach, as well as in its internal relations. It proceeds by continuous variation of concepts and problems, constantly going back to an earlier point to insert it in a new sequence, and spreads like a rhizome rather than branching out from roots or building up from foundations.

Nevertheless there are intense periods of invention. One follows the study of Hume when Deleuze was employed preparing students for national exams in philosophy in Gaullist France. In the early essays on Bergson from this period, much can already be found that would unfold in the remarkable series of books Deleuze would publish in the 1960s on Nietzsche, Proust, Spinoza, and Bergson. The many paths of this first moment of invention are then brought together in two great works of logic—*Difference and Repetition* and *Logic of Sense*. The events of

1968 mark a second intensive moment of invention, as Deleuze came to teach in the "experimental" department of philosophy of the University of Paris at Vincennes. There is the work with Foucault on *Groupe d'information sur les prisons* (G.I.P.) and its publication *L'Intolérable;* there is the start of his seminar at Vincennes, where the classical "progressivity of knowledge" was abandoned, and the doors opened to an increasingly "diverse" public, comprising many nonphilosophers drawn to his philosophy; and above all there is the experiment in "multiple authorship" and "pop philosophy" with Félix Guattari, leading to the publication in 1980 of *A Thousand Plateaus,* the book Deleuze was to consider his best and most inventive. In these ways, Deleuze's brand of philosophical empiricism joined forces with the kind of "gay science" the forces of 1968 seem to release—rather as the new empiricism of Feyerabend and Kuhn, in opposition to the "image of science" inherited from logical positivism, would accompany the release of similar forces in America. It is this phase in his work for which Deleuze is best known; and he was never to go back on it, as with those in France inclined to "postmodernism."

For in fact the moment was no longer right for *A Thousand Plateaus,* and Deleuze was disappointed with its reception. In the 1980s we then find a third moment of invention in the unfolding of Deleuze's philosophy. The question of empiricism is found in the identification of a new problem, which, on several occasions, he would come to present as our problem today—the problem of belief in the world. It receives its fullest development through Deleuze's study of the way cinema after the war introduced a new kind of relation between seeing, time, and action, starting with the attempt to "show the intolerable" on finds in neo-Realism. The problem had already been raised in

Difference and Repetition, in the passages in which Deleuze introduces his commentary on Hamlet's phrase "the time is out of
joint," and the way it might be applied to Kant.[19] There Deleuze
says that the role of belief in the "synthesis of time" geared to unknown futures, or to what is yet to come, was best formulated by
religious philosophers like Kierkegaard, Pascal, and Péguy. For
in relation to their respective religions they replaced the question of belief in God with a question of the mode of existence of
the believer, pointing the way to another kind of conversion: a
belief or trust placed in this world rather than in an another,
transcendent one. It is this kind of "empiricist conversion" that
Deleuze then thinks the "time-images" in cinema offered us, after Hitler and the war. The problem it worked out together with
postwar philosophy was a whole crisis in "movement"—for example, in the "dialectical montage" and the movement of the
masses to self-consciousness in which Eisenstein could still put
his trust. The whole relation of thought to action or agency had
to change; the problem of "representing the masses" would be
rethought in relation to the space and time of minorities in accordance with a new pragmatism, a new empiricism in relation
to the world or to trust in the world. But in formulating this
problem in his study of cinema, Deleuze identified a new rival
to it, that of information or communication; and in a short essay, he would go on to sketch the "mutation in capitalism" that
goes with it, posing different kinds of problems than the ones
Foucault had diagnosed in his analysis of disciplines.[20] It is a feature of "control" in such societies to again take the world from
us; and so we need a fresh "empiricist conversion" to restore trust
in the world and the relation of philosophy to it. In a last or late
moment of invention Deleuze then turned to the question of

imagining what philosophy is, and so might be, to take on this new rival, this new problem.

5

Deleuze was a peculiarly generous philosopher, attracted to the theme of the "virtue that gives" in Nietzsche, to the point where it is sometimes difficult to separate his originality from those he wrote about or with whom he collaborated. He was not given to polemic, preferring instead to push things in the directions he favored—even in the case of Kant. In *Logic of Sense* he writes of the peculiar sort of generosity that consists in giving what can only be "stolen"—thus suggesting a somewhat different notion of *philia* or friendship than the "giving what one doesn't have" by which Lacan had defined love. In fact, many ideas would thus be "stolen" from Deleuze by philosophers and nonphilosophers alike, with respect to which he nevertheless maintained a re-markable equanimity. For he was a philosopher unusually free from the habitual circuit of envy, paranoia, and "anxiety of influence" (or Oedipal complex) surrounding the invention and "possession" of ideas. He was ever on the lookout for what is new or singular in others; and he tried to encourage "uses" while dis-couraging "interpretations" of his philosophy by others. One might even say that such generosity belongs to his peculiar *ethos* or "manner of existence" in doing philosophy, and fits with the empiricism that tries to push beyond judgment to an invention and affirmation that precedes it—to that point where experi-mentation in philosophy becomes inseparable from a vitalism.

To learn, to impart philosophy was then to be brought to have this experience, to engage in this experimentation, for which there exists no method, no doctrine, no School, only a kind of "friendship." Even in the tradition Deleuze was drawn to misfits and mavericks like the hapless Peirce, the mad Nietzsche, the joyful Spinoza, or the superficial Lucretius, difficult to digest in official histories of philosophy. For him philosophy had no Party, no Church, no Avant-garde. He was never a Marxist nor an anti- or post-Marxist; rather he tried to take up Marx's problems in an altered context, asking what it would mean, beyond the claims of a Party, to "represent the masses," to analyze capitalism in terms of the "immanence" of other possibilities of life, and our capacity to experiment with them. In the end, he found there was still too much transcendence, mysticism, or "allegory" in using the term "utopian" for such possibilities; he preferred Samuel Butler's "erehwon," anagram of "nowhere" and "now here," secret of a kind of empiricism, which rejoins the "Englishness" of Hume's original notion of convention.[21]

For what Deleuze admired in Hume is that, along with Spinoza, he departed from the assumptions of the classical contract theory of society, pointing ahead to a view of society as experiment, in accordance with the formulation of a new problem—that of the violence inherent in identity or identification as such. Such was the import of Hume's problem of our "partialities" to family, clan, or nation—a problem more intractable than that of a rational or equitable ordering of interests, which Hume sought to resolve through an "artifice" in the composition of our passions (or through a kind of "civility"). In Spinoza the problem would rather assume to the form, beyond any "politico-theology," of an immanence of other powers in the composition of ourselves as singular essences, or in terms of the triumph of joyful over sad passions in the city. For Spinoza thought the worst and most intractable hatred or violence is the one that comes from devotion and is perpetuated in its name. It is then in such passions and processes, rather than in interests and their organization, that Deleuze's peculiar empiricism or experimentalism discovers its supposition and its address. It does not appeal to us as mutually recognizable subjects of the sort we might imagine emerging from nature to constitute society, but rather as a kind of as yet indefinite or inchoate "multitude," prior to the "constitution" of societies, singular, unformed, without myths or "majority" models or histories, yet to be invented. It is in its appeal to such a "people to come," to such a belief "in the future, of the future"—in the unknown knocking at the door—that philosophy would find the element of its experience; and it is in pushing it to this point that Deleuze's empiricism becomes the secret of a philosophy.

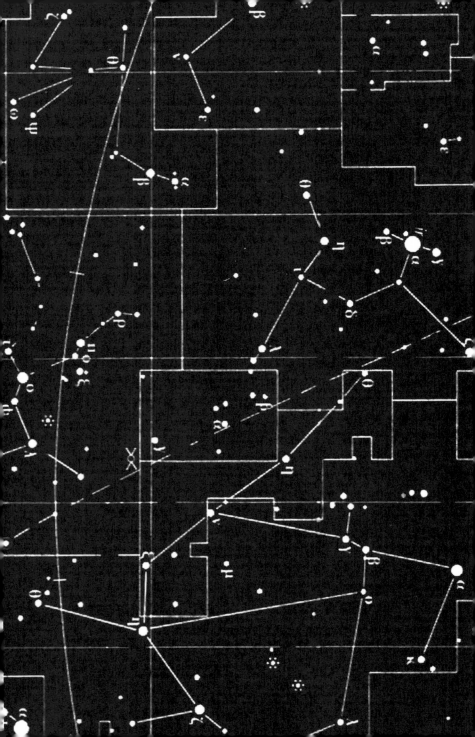

3: *Thought*

1

Deleuze was a philosopher who thought that philosophies are singular creations. Each philosopher creates *a* philosophy, indefinite enough for there to be others. The idea of philosophy is thus not fixed— there is no one method, no one way of doing it. Rather each philosophy invents a distinctive *agon* with its own *dramatis personae:* in each we find what Deleuze comes to call an "image of thought," even if the image is not always obvious. In setting up its image—sometimes in dramatically shifting from one image to another—each philosopher recasts what it means to think, or, in Foucault's words, starts to "think in other ways." But the idea that what matters in philosophies are "images of thought" is, of course, a supposition of Deleuze's own philosophy and what he extracts from the tradition; it is a concept he devises in his own search for new ways, new styles of doing philosophy. Found in his earliest writings, the idea receives its name in a section of his study of Proust, where Deleuze offers an original rethinking of the image in Plato. Later he makes it the object of the pivotal chapter in his book *Difference and Repetition,* and later further elaborates it in his striking contrast between a sprawling rhizome and a tree branching from roots; in *What Is Philosophy?* he then goes on to discuss why the creation of concepts in philosophy always supposes such an image.

What then is an "image of thought"? It is not a picture or representation of something; it is not a *Weltanschaung,* but has another more complicated "untimely" relation to its time. It can never be simply deduced from the contexts or concepts of a philosophy; instead it is a tacit presupposition of the creation of concepts and their relation to what is yet to come. There is no method to arrive at it and it is never completely explicit; rather it emerges in tandem with creation of concepts in a philosophy

as partially obscure or unexplicated partnar. It requires a peculiar art of seeing, not to be confused with a "transparency"
of Forms or ideas, or with "getting clear" about propositions
or theses—even the "exceptional clarity" of Hume, Deleuze
thinks, is not about ideas, but relations, and thus points to what
is yet to come.[1] It works from "intuitions" about problems
rather than propositions, and is thus akin to what Wittgenstein
had in mind in his preference for exposing "pictures" over advancing or disputing arguments, or when he declares "don't
think, look!" For the problems in philosophy are such that they
can be "seen" from the angles of other new philosophies, so that,
as with Wittgenstein, one can be shown a way out of them. An
art of seeing or showing the problems of philosophy goes with
the construction of images of thought. And yet in philosophy
there have also existed illusions about such images and the relations of concepts to them. Instead of a tacit supposition the image has been turned into something that itself might be derived
from concepts. It has been made a matter of seeing the "first entities" from which all would derive—to seeing the Forms, arriving at clear and distinct ideas, or exposing interpretive contexts
or relations to epochs. Taken together, such illusions belong to
what in *Difference and Repetition* Deleuze calls the "dogmatic image of thought," and a basic aim of his philosophy is to dissipate
these illusions, to expose this dogmatism.

From quite early on, Deleuze insisted that philosophical concepts are created or "fabricated" and not found in some preexistent heaven, and that this fabrication comes in response to
problems that, far from being resolved once and for all, are
themselves constantly being recast, reformulated, or "dissolved"
from new perspectives such that one can say that the problems
always persist in the solutions given to them. Creating new

concepts in response to such problems is then to be distinguished from contemplation of first entities, reflection on first ideas, or establishing intersubjective roles of rational discussion; it has other aims and makes suppositions rebellious to such "illusory" images. But the illusions that have thus restricted the creation of concepts in philosophy to first entities, given methods, or intersubjective rules are not themselves simply false propositions; and to dissipate them is more than to correct an error—otherwise, "setting up" an image could after all be obtained by a method of correcting propositional errors. Instead Deleuze likens the illusions to "mirages of thought," or to a "thick fog" thrown up in order, in a given situation, to carry on the activity of creating concepts and of "seeing" problems; and to combat them he invents an original practice he calls "nooology" or the study of images of thought. For example, as we have seen, Deleuze thinks Hume shifts the image of philosophy from combating errors to exposing "illusions" induced by the "relations" constitutive of thought or given by human nature. In taking up this idea, Kant would then identify a new kind of illusion—the "transcendental illusion," which arises when one goes beyond the legitimate bounds of thought. But the difficulties of "transcendental-empirical doubling" expose an illusion inherent in this view itself or with the very image of philosophy as a judge or watchman at the bounds of reason; the solution is then found in a new image in which thought becomes concerned with an experimentation with what is not yet given within any such bounds or comes from outside such limits. In turning to this image one then arrives at what Deleuze considers to be the source or matrix of the previous illusions. In *Difference and Repetition,* Deleuze had been above all concerned with illusions of "representation"—the notion that there exists, in a large sense, a "mimetic" link between first entities (or clear ideas) and their instantiations (of objects) would be the source of the "error" whose "fable" Nietzsche had famously told, or again of what James ridiculed as the "copy theory of truth." To this Deleuze would add an illusion of "discourse" (confusing problems—and the seeing of problems—with propositions and theses); an illusion of "the eternal" (forgetting that concepts are created or produced, not found) and of "the universal" (thinking that first entities or clear ideas explain things, when they themselves are always just what needs to be explained as fresh perspectives emerge). But in *What Is Philosophy?* he proposes to see all these illusions as themselves variants on a great illusion of "transcendence," which arises when one reintroduces first entities or ideas onto a "plane of immanence" supposed by a philosophy, making it an immanence *to* something prior, subjective or objective.[2] Philosophy becomes truly experimental or attains its "radical empiricism" only when it dissipates the illusion of transcendence in all its variants—only then does it free itself from the "dogmatic image of thought."

As the study of "images of thought," noo-ology thus turns out to be a rather subtle art. It doesn't try to work out once and for all *the* "plane of immanence" for all philosophy; rather in each philosophy it tries not only to identify a peculiar image of thought but also to clear away the fogs of transcendence that surround it, and to reestablish the moment of originality in its "creations." Thus Plato, for example, is seen to in fact *create* the concept of "the Forms" rather than finding it in a higher realm, or remembering it from a preexistence (as the illusion of "contemplation" would have us believe); and that singular creation in turn supposes an image of thought in which friends or *philoi* are brought together in a new kind of contest or *agon* in the city surrounding an original problem—how to derive everything from pure models or the "imitation" of prior unchanging or intact originals. The priority of this problem or this *agon* over the "illusions of contemplation" it secretes can then be worked out in a number of ways. It is betrayed by a kind of aporetic line running through the *Dialogues* concerning the question of *pseudos* in the *Theatetus,* of *philia* in the *Pheadrus* and *Symposium,* and of the *chora* in the *Timaeaus;*[3] and following this line we start to discern a new problem to be developed or "seen" by others—that of the "simulacra" that can't be made to participate in the pure Forms or the hylomorphic schemes they suppose. Thus we find the swerves of Lucretius's atoms, or again, in Plotinus, the problem of the "unparticipatable" or "un-imitatable" already be posed in relation to a "complication" in things (thus anticipating Proust or Liebniz); and new images and illusions of thought arise. In dispelling those illusions, noo-ology in each case tries to show that what purports to be a universality of contemplation, reflection, or communication in fact only derives from an image of thought that grows up around a particular problem and corresponds to a particular *agon.* We then arrive at an original problem in Deleuze's own philosophy, which he formulates in *Difference and Repetition* in this way: what would it then mean to *start* philosophy "undogmatically," or with an image that secretes no illusions of transcendence; what would it mean to think without—and without the need for—any "Urdoxa"?[4]

In Deleuze's answer, there is a question of priorities or what one puts first. Deleuze thinks that *before* it tries to find a fixed method or seek a truth, a philosophy is always "oriented" (to use Kant's term), though not logically determined, by an image that supplies it with pragmatic suppositions or helps determine its modes of address. Indeed that is why a philosophy always works out the intuition of its problems through a characteristic drama or through the invention of "conceptual personae." For example, Descartes had an intuition of what in the new physics didn't fit with Scholasticism; and to work it out he invented a new drama in philosophy, in part adapted from the Meditation form established by the Jesuits. In Descartes's *agon,* there emerges a new conceptual persona: an Idiot who prefers a rational language like French, which anyone can understand to learned Latin. Deleuze finds this to be an original figure (even if anticipated by Nicolas de Cusa), for, departing from the Scholastic definition of man as rational animal, it serves to dramatize something that is unlearned, untutored in philosophy—something that anyone, using the right "method," may discover through a "natural light."[5] But this new persona and its *lumière* at the same time expose a tacit assumption in Descartes's attempt to make the cogito or "I think" the first or presuppositionless starting point of philosophy—namely, the assumption of a "common sense" of which Descartes would declare that it is the thing most evenly distributed in the world. Thus a new persona would arise to dispense with the noo-ological postulate of common sense in turn, and approach instead the condition of what of the figure in Russian literature also called an Idiot or unlearned thinker. In philosophy, we start to see a Russian rather than a Cartesian Idiot, who, in his departure from learning, no longer needs to suppose that he is only discovering what anyone might be brought to see by a natural light; he starts instead to look for something conceptually foreign even in a "natural language" like French—one example Deleuze gives is Nietzsche's dream to write in Polish or to make philosophical German "dance." With such Idiots, the pragmatic presuppositions of philosophy shift, revealing new relations between "private" and "public." One example (not mentioned by Deleuze) might be Wittgenstein, always ill at ease with his public professorship and with the emergence of a new analytic "Scholasticism," who declared "the philosopher is a citizen of no circle of ideas; that is just what makes him a philosopher."[6] Indeed in both of his phases Wittgenstein was a very much a philosopher concerned with what Deleuze calls the "image of thought"—it is rather as if the Russian Idiot would become sick with the endless "false problems" induced by language, even if he still dreams of an "ordinary language" into which they might be dissolved or that might at last be purified of them. In *Difference and Repetition* Deleuze says in effect that the only way to "start without presuppositions" in philosophy is to become some sort of Russian Idiot, giving up the presumptions of common sense, throwing away one's "hermeneutic compass" and instead trying to turn one's "idiocy" into the "idiosyncrasies" of a style of thinking "in other ways."

For what Russian Idiots show is not only that philosophical thought is unlearned, but also that it is free in its creations not when everyone agrees or plays by the rules, but on the contrary, when what the rules and who the players are is not given in advance, but instead emerges along with the new concepts created and the new problems posed. Such Idiots help dramatize, in other words, what is "pragmatically supposed" by a philosophy that no longer even purports to be derived from fixed methods or prior forms, that is instead content to work out its peculiar problems, at first given by intuition, by creating concepts that then become tied up with others in many complicated ways, in a manner suggested by an adage of Leibniz that Deleuze was fond of quoting: one thinks one is at port only to discover that one is in fact still at sea.

2

The aim of Deleuze's "noo-ology" was, then, to point to new "undogmatic" ways of doing philosophy. We may distinguish three basic ways in which this aim was pursued.

1. First, noo-ology takes the place in Deleuze of the history of philosophy, not only in its textbook version, but also in the more "philosophical" ones we find in Hegel or Heidegger—the history of Spirit or of Being. Deleuze's "image of thought" is thus not to be confused with a "precomprehension of Being" any more than a *Gestalt* or "sphere" of Spirit; and, and in disputing the historicism Hegel and Heidegger tried to introduce into the image of thought, Deleuze declares that there is no great plot in the sequence of philosophies—no "intrinsic narrative."[7] It is more as in cinema a matter of juxtaposing or superimposing many different layers in a montage; for, instead of narrative— before narrative—philosophies have a kind of "stratigraphic time." Thus philosophy does not in fact divide up into epochs, go in circles, either dialectical or hermeneutical; and it does not confront us as a Destiny of the West or as a Universal History. Nor is it instead a long argument in which one side triumphs over the other with the better argument, or a long "conversation" that converts new ideas into agreements, such that what is now novel or singular later becomes what is accepted. Rather there is a sense in which what is new in philosophy remains so— indeed it belongs precisely to the "paidea" of studying past philosophers to show what is still new in them. Thus in Deleuze's studies, each philosopher emerges with fresh features as a kind of "contemporary," in the process exposing new connections between or across strata (Spinoza joins hands with Nietzsche and Lucretius). For the contemporary moment that links

Deleuze's studies together is an "untimely" one in which, as it were, established strata start to shift, opening up new fault lines and possibilities, through which older conceptual personae mutate and reappear in new guises as in what Foucault called Deleuze's "philosophical theater."[8]

In his noo-ology Deleuze thus tried to free philosophy and the "time" of philosophizing from the whole idea of epochs, and so from portentious images like the self-realization of Spirit or "Destining" of the West, as well as from more complacent ones like the long conversation issuing in agreement, and to look for another sort of image. He sensed that ours was a moment in which we *could* no longer tell ourselves the great stories recounted first by Hegel, then Heidegger, or make them intrinsic to the act of thinking, and that "our" problem lay elsewhere, in a process through which "Europe" itself was becoming something else, thereby exposing new relations with other places—with America and Russia in the nineteenth century, as well as with many "non-Western" forms of thought, such as the one Levinas had sought in Judaism.[9] Indeed one might say it was Deleuze's intuition that we might now see philosophy as having—or as having had—*no* intrinsic historical "home" or "land" or "civilization," and that we might then rethink its geographies and borders in terms of an odd potential that keeps arising in different times and places, released through many circumstances and contingencies. Thus in his "geophilosophy" Deleuze says that philosophy *might* well have started elsewhere than in Athens and with Plato, for, instead of origins, philosophy has only a "milieu" or "atmosphere," favored by certain conditions such as those provided by the "colonizing democracy" of Athens, which brought itinerant strangers into its agora to encounter Socrates.[10] Such conditions—permitting at once the *doxa, philia,* and a sense of "immanence" required to invent a philosophy—would then be re-united again in Europe through the rise of modern capitalism, the image of *philia,* for example, emerging from Christian themes of "brotherhood." The philosophies invented in such circumstances or under such conditions are then themselves the property of nowhere and no-one—not because philosophy appeals to some eternal or supervenient Republic of Spirits (of the sort suggested by the various "illusions" of philosophy), but rather, more basically, because it must always be set up or insti-tuted (*instaurer*) anew, without presuppositions as to the "we" it thereby creates or the "publics" it incites, or the new milieu in which it may start up again from a new angle.

Deleuze goes on to analyze the various "nationalitarianisms" and "utopianisms" in the images of thought in the last century in terms of this "unlanded" sense of philosophy and philosophi-cal geographies, or in terms of his own idea of "erehwon"—of the "nowhere" that is "now here."[11] In his image, in other words, there is always a moment of "absolute deterritorialization" in the invention of a philosophy, which cannot then be covered over or compensated by the "imagined community" of a given nation or utopian condition, and so calls for the invention of other new "territories." With this "deterritorialized" or "unlanded" view of philosophical geographies there goes a second principle in Deleuze's noo-ology—that there is no "imperium of truth" in philosophy, and no need to postulate one in order to think phil-osophically. On the contrary, we need to extract the *agon* of philosophical friends from illusory images of an ideal city, a transcendent law, a prior contract, or an original humanity, and say rather, with the excommunicated Marrano Spinoza, that a city is free and vital to the degree that it allows for the move-ment of free thought, and for the "peoples" such philosophical movement creates and brings together, the more and more diverse the better.

2. Such movement always has an "outside." We have already seen that Deleuze admired the way Sartre created an outside to the Sorbonne, as later would Foucault, as a "new archivist in the city"—that is what would make each a "private thinker" and not simply a "public professor." For "private" in this case doesn't mean "internalized" or "subjective," but on the contrary is defined by an "outside" that supplies philosophy other sorts of pragmatic suppositions than those enshrined in the Kantian tradition that would tie together the University and the *Rechstaat*.[12] More generally, in Deleuze's noo-ology there is an attempt to free the image of the *philoi* in philosophy from the need to identify ourselves or recognize one another according to some higher law or contrary or republic—to free the image of being "friends of the concept" from an identification of an ideal or transcendent sort, and instead make itself part of an "experimentation" in philosophy with this "we" that is not given, or that makes us "strangers to ourselves." Each of the "personae" through which a philosophy dramatizes its ideas suggests a manner in which philosophy is oriented and the kind of struggle in which it is thus involved.

Plato invents the persona of Socrates and his *agon* with the Sophists; Kant instead imagines a Judge watching over the bounds of reason; Leibniz casts himself rather as a defense attorney for God in a world that seems to have abandoned him, ever adducing new principles, while Spinoza, in giving up even such a God, creates instead the persona of an Innocent, a "sort of child-player against whom one can do nothing."[13] In each case we have different ways the contest or "game" of philosophy is played and its adversaries defined. In Deleuze's noo-ology, such images are prior to the sorts of truth philosophies have sought and the ways they have gone about it, and thus, "the relation to truth in philosophy is neither stable nor constant, which is why it can't be used to define it."[14] Socrates said the wicked man deceives himself, but what precisely is such "self-deception"—is it, for example, the same thing as Sartrian *"mauvaise foi,"* or Lukacsian "false consciousness," or is it rather more like the "totalitarian lie" against which Soviet-bloc "dissident" philosophies were directed? Perhaps it is not quite any of these. For what matters is not a single unchanging "relation to truth" but rather, the different ways the relation is oriented and its particular friends, foes, and rivals determined. There have been many kinds of truth in philosophy and many ways of saying it; and in analyzing the images of thought that underlie them Deleuze tries to show how philosophies and philosophers have been called upon to do different things—to enlighten, emancipate, instruct, transport, transform, civilize, guard or challenge the state, and so forth. One might then say there is a sense in which the image of thought, and of what thought is called on to combat, is prior to "argument" in a philosophy, such than one might analyze styles of argument in relation to the orientations they receive through such images. Thus Descartes would "argue" in a different way than did Plato or Hume or Wittgenstein or Kant—through "meditations" rather than "dialogues," "inquiries," "investigations," or "critiques"—as well as from the tendency in analytic philosophy to argue in accordance with a litigious image of lawyers preparing a brief, advancing and justifying claims, finding precedents, making a case.

But this priority of images with respect to "relations of truth" in philosophy is not a relativism; on the contrary, it forms part of the process of "selection" through which Deleuze attempts to rid thought of its "dogmatic image." In *Difference and Repetition* the selection among images of thought is made in this way: a given image is understood in relation to its "negative," or what it is directed against (e.g., error, superstition, ideology, etc.); and an image is freed from the dogmatic presuppositions of the sort shown in Descartes's appeal to common sense (or by the Cartesian Idiot) to the degree that it no longer takes as its negative an error to be corrected, or an ideology to be overcome, but rather a stupidity or *bêtise* to be exposed and attacked. A truly presuppositionless philosophy, in other words, would be the one the *agon* of which would not derive from, and be directed against, ideational or propositional error (as with a "discourse on method"), but rather would take on a prior and more intractable stupidity. In the nineteenth century, Flaubert proposed such stupidity as that which literature would be concerned to attack and from which it derives, thus supplanting the more classical problems of error and fiction; and Deleuze finds that within philosophy Nietzsche would define a similar task, later taken up by Foucault—*nuire à la bêtise,* to harm or attack stupidity.[15] As a term for the element in which the philosophical agon is carried on, "stupidity" is not "irrationality," even though it is done at the cost of a certain "madness," and involves the thinker in a relation to something inhuman or intolerable. Rather what it involves is that philosophy starts not in some naturally given desire to know, or in accordance with a "natural light" (as traditionally supposed), but rather with the encounter with something that doesn't fit in habitual ways of seeing and thinking, that "shakes up" thinking and puts up something new to be thought. If there is something *bête* (at once stupid and bestial) about thinking, it is precisely because it can't rely on the sunny "good will" of knowing, and must rather work with the shock of something for which there exists no prior learning, method, or knowledge, and so with the "bad will" or "resistance" to habitual ways of thinking that the intuition of such a shock induces in one. For it is such "problematization" that pushes the philosopher (and his friends) "outside" *doxa* without necessarily affording the assurances of a superior or first knowledge, or something everyone will be brought to see and agree upon; and that is just why thinking in terms of "problematizations" is such a "perilous activity," fraught with many risks or dangers. To attack a stupidity is then not the same thing as to correct an error, dispel a superstition, or critique an ideology—it is not exactly a "demystification" and supposes no higher science. The aim is rather to make new forces visible, formulating the problems they pose, and inciting a kind of experimental activity of thinking around them; for, as Foucault puts it, the opposite of stupidity is not intelligence, but rather thinking or philosophy itself.[16] In his noo-ology, Deleuze thus offers more than a sense of the variety of "relations to truth" in philosophy. At the same time, with his image of stupidity as the "negative" of thought, he suggests what it would mean, in carrying on philosophy, to put one's trust not in some transcendence or *Urdoxa,* but rather in the world from which thinking derives and in which it becomes effective.

3. This priority of "images of thought" with respect to history or narrative in philosophy, and to the different kinds of "relations to truth" it sets up, in turn alters the kinds of relations philosophy is thought to have with other disciplines, notably, the sciences and the arts. Dispelling the illusions of "representation" or the "intrinsic narrative of philosophy," for example, has consequences for the way art and science have traditionally been

conceived, or for their philosophical understandings of themselves. Deleuze's conception of the "image of thought," in other words, leads to a new "image of science" or new "image of art" in philosophy; and a third aim in his noo-ology is then to work out the kinds of relations philosophy would then have with these other disciplines.

There are two pictures he thinks we need to get away from. The first is an image of supervenience—an image of philosophy as a metadiscipline that sets or keeps the rules for the others, as when an attempt is made to set down a method to "appraise theories" in science, or a "theory of judgment" for the arts. Deleuze thinks that not only do artists and scientists have no need of philosophers for appraisal or judgment in their domains, but that scientific methods and forms of judgment themselves evolve in ways that can't be foreseen in advance. The relations of philosophy with arts or sciences are then to be sought in another direction. Deleuze sees no reason why the tradition of "natural philosophy" of the sort exemplified by Whitehead's cosmology should not be continued, perhaps in relation to new speculations about chaos or complexity; and in this regard, he admires, for example, Michel Serres's study of mathematical models in Leibniz or Stoic physics, or his attempt to work out "translations" of thermodynamical ideas in the arts. He also sees no reason why a philosophical problem like how we and our world are determined in space and time should not be explored in a medium like cinema, or extracted from it. With such "resonances and interferences," however, it is important to dispel a second picture—that of a kind of identification or imitation. We find this picture in both "positivist" and "aestheticist" forms in modern philosophy—Quine's attempt to "naturalize" philosophy would be an example of the first, attempts to "textualize" philosophy as "literary theory" by literature professors would be an example of the second. One reason Deleuze found talk of "antiphilosophy" or "postphilosophy" so tiresome is that, in contrast to such views, he always took philosophy to have its "own raw materials which allow it to enter into external relations—which are all the more necessary—with other disciplines."[17] He thought that philosophy deals with different sorts of problems than do the arts or sciences, which survive their first formulations or persist in the first solutions given to them, even if there exist zones where one can't yet say whether a given problem will turn out to be philosophical, artistic, or scientific. Such problems and "problematizations" require that one think where one cannot know with scientific assurance, and yet they are not irrational, illogical, or unscientific; rather they have their own consistency, and are best connected with that element of the unknown which the growth of science always carries with it and the kinds of "sensations" that the arts keep extracting from recognizable things and the mental habits associated with them. For such are the kinds of "external relations" that become all the more necessary when philosophy for its part gives up its pretense to some *Urdoxa* or higher knowledge, and turns instead to its peculiar problems, the events that give rise to them, the intuitions through which they take form, and the effects they have on previous ways of thinking, and so "attacks stupidity" in the lives of people.

Along such lines, Deleuze's noo-ological investigations would lead him to the "practical" question of actually doing philosophy in a nondogmatic or presuppositionless manner; it would become a matter of the "thinking in his own right," which he says above all reading Nietzsche inspired in him. Pursuing this inspiration, doing philosophy under this image, would then take Deleuze to the great questions of logic, life, and art.

4: *Multiplicity*

1

In Deleuze, "logic" acquires a new sense. It is called upon to do new things suited to the "image of thought" he tries to work out: a logic of "multiplicity," a logic of sense. For those who take "logic" to mean a sentential calculus of truth, his notion may well seem paradoxical or nonsensical; those who want a method of inference for the sciences may well not recognize it as a logic at all. To correct errors in inference, it may be useful to have a calculus or method. But to get away from the illusions of recognition and representation in thought and to be able to think in other ways, one needs a logic of another kind. Indeed one must dispel the illusion that problems in thought reduce to the sort of question that can be resolved once and for all by deriving propositions from others taken as premises—a variant of what Deleuze calls "the discursive illusion." He thinks that there is always a prior question of determining what a true—and what a false—problem is: "The category of sense replaces that of truth when true and false describe the problem and not the propositions that respond to it."[1] Inspired by empiricism, his would be "a logic of sense and event" rather than "a logic of predication and truth."[2] But what kind of logic is this? It is unlike Kant's "transcendental" logic, or Hegel's "dialectical" one; Deleuze is drawn instead to the role of Ideas in Kant, and he underscores that the sense and logic of difference is "nondialectizable." It presupposes another view of philosophy itself: "I conceive of philosophy as a logic of multiplicities," declares Deleuze at one point.[3] The question of Deleuze's logic is then what it might mean to think in terms of multiplicities rather than identities or propositions, and so to see ourselves, and our brains, as composed of multiplicities rather than predicates and the propositions into which they enter.

Deleuze's logic is thus concerned not with the "recognition of the true," but with another problem, another conception of problems—to show and work out the "complications" in our thinking. It is a logic of the "creation of concepts" that derive from problematizations, and it has other pragmatic presuppositions and aims than a logic that says how to move from some true sentences to others, or to pass from indetermination to a dialectical whole, or to arrive at a priori categories of thought. If conceived as a machine, it would not be not a calculating or computing machine—a Turing machine—but rather a sort of "complicating" machine, moving between usual distinctions, surprising us, attaining an irreducible disparity, an incalculable chance, more akin to Alfred Jarry's "tempo-mobiles" than Jerry Fodor's "modules."[4] Indeed it leads Deleuze to another view of the brain and cognition than the kind of artificial intelligence that serves only to go back to "the most stubborn logic" of recognition and representation.[5]

Despite—or perhaps just because of—such peculiarities, Deleuze's logic is about the relations between thinking and life itself. Indeed it is precisely a "practical" question about life that Deleuze tries to extract from the philosophical tradition. In *Logic of Sense,* for example, he offers a highly original view of the Stoic logic of implication in terms of "sense and event" rather than "truth and proposition," in which, along with Stoic physics, it becomes the logic for the great practical question of how to accept fate while refusing necessity, and, more generally, of how "not to be unworthy of what happens to us."[6] Similarly, his analysis of the logic of Substance and its modes in Spinoza's *Ethics* as a logic of "immanence" and the "singularities" that compose it leads to a "practical philosophy" (as distinct from a morality) that recasts the relation of thought (especially in its appeal to "common notions") to life.[7] In the case of Bergson, he proposes to introduce a "conception of difference" into the life, its *élan* and its "creative evolution"; the result is a logic of "indetermination" prior to organistic or purposive form, shown rather in a sort of "pragmatism" of perception, memory, and action. In each case Deleuze's logic leads to his vitalism, and his vitalism to his logic. There is much humor, play, and ruse in Deleuze's logic, which comes from the vital exercise in thought, the "practical philosophy," from which it is inseparable.

To understand Deleuze's logic is then to understand the "sense" of which—in which—it is a logic. For it is neither a method of inference for scientists (something of which Deleuze thinks they have no need), nor a syntax for computers (whose relations to thinking must be understood in other ways). It is a logic of a "sense" prior to established "truth-values" and public agreements, or prior to "I think" or "we think," always ramifying or proliferating in unexpected ways. It is a logic for thinking not in terms of generalities and particularities, but rather in terms of singular ideas, complications and "complex themes"— not in terms of identities and oppositions but rather of "differences" over which we can't quantify and interstices between given distinctions or with what is not yet and never completely "ontologically determined." It is neither deductive nor inductive—it is not even propositional; rather it is the logic for a kind of conceptual art to deal with what is problematic and complicating in what happens to us. It is, in other words, a logic for an experience and activity of thought that is deformed or obscured when reduced to a theory of inference of the sort we see in Aristotle's syllogisms. On the contrary, it tries to free thinking from the "poisoned gift"[8] of transcendence that Plato introduced into thought when he imagined everything to be only the imitation of pure Forms, as well as the various guises this gift and this poison would assume in "transcendental," "dialectical," and "symbolic" logics. We must "reverse Platonism" (as Plato himself was in fact the first to do)—only then do we see what logic is and can do.

2

We must "track down" the illusion of transcendence in Plato as Plato himself tried to track down the Forms, extracting them from the sensorial imperfection of things.[9] At the heart of the illusion, Deleuze finds the logic of the relations of the Forms to their "instantiations"—the logic of universal and particular, and type and token, and the corresponding operations of generalization and specification, leading to the sort of treelike or taxonomic view of "categories" that haunted Aristotle. Today such relations and operations tend to be understood following Frege, in terms of sets and their members with functions mapping one onto the other. But for Deleuze this Fregean view only compounds the illusion in Plato's gift, perpetuating the confusion of philosophical problems with propositions. His own "logic of multiplicities" adopts another principle adapted from the critique of abstractions in Whitehead: the abstract doesn't explain; it must itself be explained by reinsertion into a multiplicity.[10]

Thus Deleuze declares the Frege-Russell view of concepts as set-functions to be "necessarily reductive"—reductive precisely of the "sense" and "complication" he wants to reintroduce into logic and the idea of "concept" in philosophy, contributing to the constrictions of the analytic "image of thought" that Russell helped to introduce.[11] He thinks we need to get away from the whole picture of sets with their discrete or atomistic members, or push Russell's intuition in his theory of "relations" beyond many-placed predicate-functions. In its place we must envisage incomplete open wholes with indeterminate components for which the mathematical distinction between discrete and continuous variation, or between rational and irrational continuities, offers a better idea than Frege's functions.[12] We may then say that, in contrast to the discrete "variety" of a set, a multiplicity is a kind of potential for bifurcation and "variation" in an open whole.

Deleuze's idea of "multiplicity" is thus not to be confused with traditional notions of "the many" or "the manifold" or "variety," and requires other kinds of logical operations. Thus in contrast to "particularity," Deleuze talks of "singularity," and in contrast to "generality," he talks of an indeterminate "plan of composition" in which singularities would coalesce or come together. He finds an example of the first in the notion of "haecceity" in Duns Scotus, while Spinoza's notion of "Substance" affords an example of the second; and in Deleuze's logical universe, there thus exists, as it were, something "smaller" than the most specified individual, larger than the most general category.[13] Similarly, what he calls "difference" is not to be confused with distinction, opposition, or contradiction, and indeed may be called "free" only when it is freed from the logic of such notions. Leibniz said two things are distinct if there exists something that is true of one and not true of the other; but even in Leibniz, Deleuze detects "differences" or "singularities" prior to such a distinction, and with another sense: two things may be said to "differ freely" when, fitting in no class, they fall together in a kind of indefinite *voisinage* or neighboring. A "singularity" is thus not an instance or instantiation of anything—it is not particularity or uniqueness. As Deleuze puts it, its individuation is not a specification; and indeed there exist individuations that are quite "impure," mixing elements from many different species. But this not-fitting-in-a-class, this "indefiniteness" or "vagueness" is not a logical deficiency or incoherence, but, rather, as with what Peirce called "firstness," it is a kind of power or chance, a "freshness" of what has not yet been made definite by habit or law.[14] Thus, as with Peirce's talk of a "heterogeneity" that comes first, Deleuze speaks of a logical "disparity" that is neither a "diversity" nor a simple disorder; he speaks of "disparation" that does not divide a space into distinct parts, but rather so disperses or scatters it to allow the chance for something new to emerge. It is then such "free differences" or "disparities" or "singularities" that make up "multiple assemblages"; that is why they have a sense given through logical "syntheses" of an original sort, quite different from "truth functions." The components of a multiplicity, unlike the members of a set, must be indefinite or vague, matching with the "vagabond" manner in which a multiplicity is constructed; and the problem in Deleuze's logic then becomes how to repeat "free differences" in complex wholes that don't reduce what makes them differences, how to connect "singularities" in a "plan of consistency" that preserves what makes them singular.

3   Deleuze's aim may then be said to elaborate this basic problem in the logic of multiplicities along four lines.

1. There is an attempt to work out logical connectives of an original sort, irreducible to generalization or specification within pure categories, hence irreducible to the combination

and intersection of sets—connectives that work rather with "zones of indistinction" that escape oppositions or contradictions. Following Blanchot, one might speak of a "neutralization" of given distinctions (from *"ne-uter,"* neither nor that), which leads not to absence but to "multiplicity," to new points of connection. It opens, in other words, the possibility of a "disjunctive synthesis," where the disjuncts are "disparate" rather than "distinct" and the synthesis "inclusive" rather than "exclusive" ("let this go with that"). Even "not" ceases to be a way of switching truth-values, or moving to the next higher stage in a dialectic, and it becomes only the mark of the actualization of a multiplicity ("not found in any given distinctions, because unfolding something else, something new"). The "implications" of philosophical concepts are then "unfolded" through such connections rather than through sets and functions, instantiations of Forms, or the attribution of predicates to a subject—unfolded, in other words, through the convergence and divergence of open or ramifying series. The basic logical operator becomes an "And," working prior to the "Is" of predication or identity.

2. With this "And," Deleuze's logic frees itself from the question of "ontological determination" (or saying what there is), as it descends from Plato's poisoned gift, or from what is found in the Quinean principle "to be is to be the value of a variable." It supposes a different kind of grammar or logical coherence than the ones modeled on sentences like "the sky is blue" or "God exists."[15] Connecting "this" and "that," moving "here" and "there," it has a different relation to language that Deleuze likens to the stammering of another language, not yet spoken, never completely understood. Only in this way can language get at what is not "ontologically determined" in our existence and our

world, what is given rather through other kinds of description, as when, in literature or in cinema, "characters" cease to be determined by fixed "qualities," but rather tied together through many bits or blocks in a logic of what happens or what has happened. For in what happens to us—and what has happened to us—there is always something "inattributable," which nevertheless forms part of our "becomings." That is what Deleuze calls an "event"—the sort of event supposed by the "sense" of his logic and the odd grammar of its "And." "In all my books I have sought the nature of the event," Deleuze declares; "it is a philosophical concept, the only one capable of destituting the verb to be and the attribute."[16]

3. This logical "destitution" is then not an end in itself, but rather the consequence of another way of thinking about and connecting things—of another kind of logical construction with a different relation to "what there is." Deleuze calls his logic "constructivist" not "deconstructionist." It is not so much about undoing identities as of putting differences together in open or complex wholes. But what then is a whole that includes multiplicity; what relations between multiple and the one are involved? As we have seen, for Deleuze a "singularity" is not something unique or *sui generis,* but, on the contrary, something that can be understood only through the ways it comes to be repeated. It precisely such "iterability of the singular" that requires a different logic than that of the generality that subsumes things in classes or the subject in which predicates inhere—the logic of a "complicated" or "complex" whole. In Deleuze's terminology, we may then say that a singularity is what enters into a "series," and a series, in contrast to a set or organic whole, is what is composed of "singularities."[17] The difference between a

series and a set or an organic whole can then be seen in the way it is continued—the way, as Deleuze puts, it is always "starting again in the middle" rather than moving from a beginning to an end.

Ludwig Wittgenstein posed the problem of continuity as a problem concerning the precise rule for adding one to a series of numbers; and Saul Kripke has shown how this problem may be extended to question of predicates, in particular, predicates used to describe ourselves, hence to Humean skepticism.[18] But unlike a series of numbers, what Deleuze calls a multiplicity can't be countered; its components can't be picked out one by one, and they retain a certain vagueness. They are rather like "stabilizations" in what Gilbert Simondon called "meta-stable systems"—systems that themselves change along with the definition of their individual components. For example, differences in color may be smaller or finer than those that fit in the sort of gross "entrenched predicates" that, for Nelson Goodman, keep "green" from turning into "grue"; and indeed it is in this way, rather than as a property of things, that Deleuze thinks color enters into the "logic of sensation" in painting.[19] In this sense, Deleuzian singularities are like "subindividual" points, prior to the worlds determined by predicates, where things may bifurcate into other "possible worlds" of predication. A multiplicity, in short, is not denumerable and must be continued in other ways—as when Wittgenstein declares of temporal continuity, that when we think of the world's future, we always mean the destination it will reach if it keeps going in the direction we can see it going now; it does not occur to us that its path is not a straight line, but a curve, constantly changing directions.[20]

Deleuze finds that the problem of continuity is better posed by Bergson, when he says that a duration is the actualization of "qualitative" rather than a "quantitative" multiplicity. To continue a multiplicity is to move into a zone that is not logically predetermined, but rather "invents by differentiating."[21] That is why duration supposes a form of time that no longer works through succession or permanence, but rather as an open whole, constantly "differentiating" and starting up again from peculiar points. Such a whole is not "organic" (expressed in each of its parts, or articulated into members working harmoniously together); and the multiplicity it brings together is not fragmentary but only uncompleted (*inachevé*) like a wall of free, uncemented stones.[22] Indeed we must get away from the exclusive alternative between organicism and mechanism—between the "holism" of the first and the "atomism" of the second. The problem instead is that of the expression of a life prior what "individualizes" us; and it is precisely such life that Deleuze tries to introduce, for example, into the logic of monads and worlds in Leibniz or find in singular modes of being and their composition in Spinoza. The "complexity" in a complex whole thus can never be reduced to simple elements and their combination, and must be "grasped" in thought in another way, through another kind of construction and continuity.

4. Philosophy is, then, a logic of multiplicity, but a multiplicity is not a set whose members can be picked out one by one. It has other sorts of "implications." Indeed one must free the notion of "implication" from problems cast in the Platonic or propositional form "what is an *X*?" For the implications of a philosophical problem are never a simple matter of inferring truths from others, but rather have another sort of relation with language: they suppose a texture or weave (*symploche*) of discourse prior to anything that might be woven from the crochets

of pure or unchanging Forms.[23] Thus Deleuze says "implications" are not consequences of theses, but rather ramifications of "complex themes," which then attach to others at various junctures or conjunctures. One picture of the "implications" of a complex theme, or of things "following" or "connecting with" one another in this informal manner, is that of series converging and diverging around problematic points. Prior to the logic of predicates and propositions, in other words, is not some great silence or void, but rather a "complication" that must be unfolded or explicated—Deleuze finds this idea of "impure complexity" of what can't be made to "participate" in the Forms adumbrated already in the neo-Platonist notion of "complicatio."

Deleuze tries to find a "Baroque" version of such complication in Leibniz, by taking up and playing with the fold or the "pli" words—implication, explication, replication, complication, "perplication."[24] Indeed that is just what makes Leibniz a philosopher of the fold or complexity, even if still contained within a preestablished harmony. Deleuze also finds the problem of pre-predicative "complication" in the problem of expression in Spinoza, and the problem of signs in Proust. In his book on Leibniz and the fold, Deleuze says a multiplicity is not what has many parts; it is what is "complicated," or folded many times over and in many ways such that there is no completely unfolded state, but only further bifurcations, as in Borges' fable of the garden of ever-forking paths. Such is the "original" sort complexity that can never be reduced to a logic of simplicity or generality. As one unfolds or explicates an implication, one is led to another, which in turn helps rethink the first while pointing to others—folds coming from folds, *plica ex plica,* as in a Baroque logic ever obliged to advance "principles." To think in terms of multiplicities is then to think with such complexity, for which

Deleuze finds a kind of "clinical" aspect expounded by Spinoza in terms of the affects and percepts of thinking.[25] There a different kind of logical "flow"—a joyful sense of "speeding up" as something singular emerges, and the depressive sense that nothing new is coming out, that one is only turning around the same impasse, unable to invent—affects rather different from the hope for a "solution" that would derive from first entities or truths, the fear of not attaining it, and the sense of self-assurance or self-importance at having gotten it.

Plato's problem was how to make everything fit into the "net" of dialectical definitions. Deleuze's logic looks for a "sieve" or "net" of another kind, prior to form-matter or hylemorphic scheme, as with the "bastard logic" of the *chora* in Plato's *Timaeus*. For his problem is how to extract what can't be made to "participate" in Forms (universals, sets, etc.), combining, assembling, "constructing" it in an incomplete informal plan, so as to be able to respond to what in life as in thought is not already determined—to those unforeseen moments in what happens in us and to us that open up onto new histories in history, new paths in the "complication" of our ways of being.

4

Deleuze's logical universe is thus populated by "differences," "singularities," and their potential complications. But there is an air of paradox in saying that there *are* or that there *exist* such "differences," so much is the idea of "being" tied up with the classical logic Deleuze is trying to get away from; and in *Logic of Sense* he calls them "extra-beings," and rather than "existing," he says that they "subsist" and "insist" in things and ourselves. One might then say of multiplicities that they "subsist" in things without our being able to specify them or to "quantify over" them—that indeed is just what makes them "qualitative." They don't fit within the "net" of a logic of quantifiers of bound variables such as "every" and "each"; a singularity is rather *quelconque,* understood as a mark of a potential or virtuality, "effectuated" in a nonquantifiable manner. We might then call Deleuze a "realist" of a peculiar sort—a realist about such virtualities that can't be forecast or foreseen, that have another relation to thought.

The philosophical problem of "realism" is often posed in what amounts to a problem of classification. Thus nominalism says only individuals exist, the classifications into which they fall being only our more or less conventional ways of sorting them, whereas essentialism says that there also exist "real" kinds or taxa. But, as we have seen, Deleuze wants to say there are indeterminate "subindividual" things that fit together in ways that are "suprageneral." Thus, for example, his question is not whether gender or sex classifications are "essential" or conventional; rather he thinks of them as "molar" categories which cover myriad "minor" becomings, the potential for which requires our "realism." Proust is a good example of this; and Deleuze thinks that what Proust called "essences" are in fact subindividual "virtualities" related to our loves and our thoughts in a much different way than the Forms of Platonic Recollection and Friendship. But it is through Bergson's distinction between the "virtual" and the "possible" that Deleuze works out the logic involved.[26] In a logic of instantiation, there is no difference between a concept and its more or less "perfect" realization, save for existence itself. By contrast, of "qualitative multiplicities" (or differences or singularities) we should rather say that they "actualize" a problematic potential that is nowhere to be found in existing logical divisions. In this case, the relation between the actual and the virtual has none of the congruity of forms and their instantiations; actualization becomes instead a matter of an "invention" of another differentiating kind, no longer contained within given logical possibilities.

But what then does it mean to be "realist" about such virtualities or the kind of invention they require? One kind of answer comes in *Cinema 2,* when Deleuze says that Italian neo-Realism was "realistic" not in its attention to social contents, but rather through the invention of a new kind of image capable of showing something "intolerable" for which there preexists no law or language of judgment. It is in this way that this realism anticipates a cinema concerned to show forces within and without, which can't be understood or "decided" in the usual way where there is no problem in distinguishing true and false, real and unreal, and so comes to a decision or judgment—a cinema that thus "sees" without knowing how to "act." But Deleuze finds the same kind of "realism" in Foucault and his art of seeing—in providing a map or diagram of the disciplines in modern societies, Foucault would be showing something intolerable that did not preexist the programs or policies; and Foucault's own talk of the time of "the actual" or "what is happening now" as point of experimentation and invention might more generally be understood to involve the realism of showing the intolerable. The principle of this realism might then be put in this way: multiplicities have the reality of "events" or of what is "inattributable" in existence, and that reality is shown in how we see them and what we do about them; thus they require that we be "realists" just where we cannot judge or decide, but only yet experiment and invent.

5

What then is the "sense" of the logic Deleuze proposes; how and where is it to be found? Like the "anonymity" that exposes discourse to "events" in Foucault, it cannot be defined by established truths and the intersubjective roles devised to attain them, but on the contrary, is presupposed by such "discursive regularities."[27] It is thus not a public sense through which we come to assign "truth-values" to sentences, or to "fix the reference" of concepts, or adopt the "propositional attitudes" that go with such activities. Deleuze's *sens* in short is not Frege's *Sinn*. It is more "original" than such *Sinn*—it "subsists and insists" in its establishment, and emerges in what Foucault called moments of its "problematization." It therefore has a different relation to "nonsense"—one can talk of things that are *unsinnig* yet not logically contradictory (like the proverbial round square), as, for example, in Foucault's talk of what in discourse is not yet or no longer a "possible truth," hence of what is not yet or no longer possible to say or see in a given regularity; and Deleuze thinks linguistically we see it as well in the "nonsense" in Lewis Carroll's fiction. What is *unsinnig* in this way is not a deficiency, but rather an essential resource of *sens*. Thus, in *Logic of Sense,* Deleuze thinks there is a virtue in that fact that in speaking I always thus express more than I can assert—something beyond the established "I think" or "we think," irreducible to performatives, public indexicalities, or the usual "persons" of discourse. He speaks of a "layer of sense" prior to the *Sinn* of propositions, references, and attitudes, which is nevertheless required by thought or by the ways things are given to be thought; it is what later, in *A Thousand Plateaus,* would lead to a "pragmatics" of language prior to the postulates of generative grammar or Saussurian *langue.* One way the priority of *sens* to propositional sense and reference is shown is, then, precisely in the peculiar sorts of problems with which philosophy is concerned—indeed it is because philosophy, like fiction, is concerned with *sens* that it always *bête,* always "paradoxical by nature." Conversely, "sense" is what is presupposed by the nature of philosophical paradox.

Analytic or "postanalytic" paradoxes given by strange terms such as "gavagai," "grue," or "twin-earth" serve to undo distinctions in the picture of sense and reference inherited from Frege, Russell, or logical positivism, even if, by Deleuze's lights, then end up restoring some form of "common sense," as in Quine's attempt to naturalize philosophy. For Bachelard, by contrast, knowledge always starts with a break with common sense, and, in taking up this idea, Foucault tried to remove such "problematization" even from Bachelard's distinction between science and ideology; in this way he arrives at the element of sense that Deleuze elaborates in his discussion of "structuralist" paradoxes in *Logic of Sense.* For they are more paradoxes of *sens* than of *Sinn.* With Lacan's "purloined letter," we are led to a problem of "complex repetition"—what we repeat in our symptoms translates into a relation to "the real" that we must distinguish not only from the problem of "representing reality" but also from the "relation to truth" found in the destinies of individuals in myth or classical narrative. In Lévi-Strauss (in his introduction to Marcel Mauss), we find the paradox of the excess of language with respect to the sense it acquires at given times and places or in given cultures or symbolic systems. This excess of language and this relation to the "real" together point to the kind of paradox or paradoxical sense Deleuze thinks is required by thinking, and of which he is proposing a logic.

The structural paradoxes help expose the ruse of the classical or dogmatic image of thought that would have us believe that outside distinction and clarity there is only confusion, chaos, or anarchy, and that outside the *Sinn* of true-or-false statements, there is only nonsense, absurdity, or silence. Deleuze wants to expose this ruse, and say that a kind of indetermination and nonsense are required for there to be thought. Thus he speaks of an indetermination that is not a blankness, void, or a dialectical night in which all cows are black, given rather through those zones of indistinction that accompany all determinations. With such indetermination he thinks there goes a "nonsense" that belongs to thought not in the manner of the existential pathos of "the absurd," but rather as this layer or zone of sense from which new things are given to be thought. Thus Deleuze thinks Socratic or Romantic "irony" still works with a negation that stays within the classical image, and in the end reinforces it; by contrast, there is a "humor," concerned rather with the relations of sense and nonsense in thought, which Deleuze finds, for example, in Hume and in Humean skepticism.

But how then is this "sense and nonsense" given to us; through what kinds of signs is it shown or indicated? Such is the basic question of Deleuze's semiotics. The problem of signs is thus rather different from the problem of symbols in symbolic logic, and indeed there is no notation in Deleuze's logic of multiplicities; rather he is always inventing new words and procedures to get at it. It is a logic for a sense (and nonsense) for which precisely there is and can be no *code.* Thus, for example, Deleuze would rebel at the idea that the unconscious is structured like a code. What Freud called "symptoms" rather serve to singularize us and our relations with one another, as if each of us had a peculiar libidinal "idiom" or "idiosyncrasy," the key to the sense of which could only be in the vagaries of what we say and do, thus creating "virtual relations" among us prior and irreducible to any symbolic order.[28] Symptoms would thus be signs of a "non-sense" that is neither error nor informational noise, but rather a prodigious impersonal reserve or virtuality of what makes of us singular beings. But how then is this strange sense for which there exists no code, no notation, no general syntax shown or expressed—how then do we "make *sens*"?

6   The problem in Deleuze's semiotics is to render this sense and so make thinkable what we have not yet been able to think, to make visible what we have been unable to discern "clearly and distinctly." It is a problem of expressing something in our modes of being that is the imitation or representation of nothing prior; and Deleuze sees it not only in Freud's "symptoms" or Proust's "signs" but also in the question of "ambiguous signs" in Leibniz or the kinds of "image" Deleuze works out in his study of cinema. In each case, signs require a different sort of intelligence than decoding a language or a logic; rather they get at something that can't be "codified"—what Deleuze calls processes of "deterritorialization" or "lines of flight." Thus Deleuze tries to envisage a semiotics that would be diagrammatic or cartographic rather than symbolic or iconic, and diagnostic of other possibilities rather than predictive or explanatory; and he talks of "abstract machines" that would thus be "diagrams" of multiplicities. For this to be possible, the notion of "sign" itself must be rethought in at least two ways.

In the first place, the relation between signs and that of which they are the signs is not governed by resemblances or fixed analogies, and it is not to be understood in terms of form and content. In the semiotics of Hjemslev, Deleuze proposes to find an informal element in expression not found in Saussure's picture of signifier and signified; or again, he takes up Husserl's notion of "infra-Euclydian" shapes, or "vague essences," that would be known with an "anexact" rigor unlike that of an axiomatic system.[29] In these ways signs would depart from the hylemorphism introduced by Plato, and work instead with a kind of "bad *mimesis*" no longer subordinated to the relation between pure originals and their instantiations—as already with "simulacra" and "phantasmata" in Plato. Thus, in the second place, in Deleuze's semiotics, there is no "double articulation"—no prior or necessary bi-univocal link between words and images or saying and seeing; there is no "schematism" as in Kant that would link intuition and concept. Thus Deleuze admired Foucault's attempt to show how the linguistico-imagistic paradoxes in Magritte serve to undo the classical representational link between words and images and so bring us an "anonymous murmur" of discourse prior to them. He sees it as part of a larger art of seeing in Foucault's archival research, where the link between what we can say and what we can see at a given time and place is fixed by discursive regularities rather than by a fixed schema. Similarly, in opposing the semiology of Christian Metz in the study of cinema, Deleuze finds a whole art of connecting words and things or discourse and vision, much as in painting, the relations between figure and discourse are obtained through varying "procedures" rather than being fixed by a scheme of representation. It is just in this way that the "sense" of cinema or painting is not a matter of code.

"Procedure" is the word Foucault uses for Deleuze's analysis of the schizophrenic world of Louis Wolfson;[30] it is a word Deleuze himself uses for Melville's formula in "Bartleby the Scrivener," "I would prefer not to." One might then think of the "signs" in

Deleuze's semiotics as such "procedures" for a universe not already prescribed by codes or coded signs, or at odds with one. They are thus "techniques" or "instruments" of a peculiar kind, which Deleuze often calls "experimental." To understand procedures we need to get away from the Platonic image of a *techne* linking form and matter, hence word and image. For we form ourselves through procedures and techniques that have another sense that can't be reduced to a common *Sinn* through which objects are represented for subjects. More generally, Deleuze thinks we need to understand instruments in terms of the larger, looser "assemblages" in which they figure together with us or our modes of being. Thus following Leroi-Gouhron's work on early material culture, Deleuze imagines a kind of evolution of instruments and the "phylums" to which they belong as involving this looser sense (e.g., does a primitive device count as a weapon or a tool?), allowing for determinations through "minor sciences" or artistic procedures or fictions.[31] Thus one might speak of a "sense" or "logic" of mechanical assemblages as distinct from the workings of actual mechanisms, and, in particular, Deleuze thinks this true for the "phylum" of informational or computational whose sense or logic tends to replace that of the mechanical. The problem of thinking with computers, or at a time of informational assemblages, should thus not be confused with the computational model of thinking or cognition. It is rather a matter of thinking in terms of this other sense, and the more "experimental" procedures it allows—a question of logical or "abstract machines" of another noncomputational kind. Thus Deleuze suggests that the information or biotechnological phyla may offer new possibilities no longer tied down to the notions of Man or of God through which the sense of "machine" or "technology" had previously been understood.[32]

7

What is a "thinking machine" or a "spiritual automaton"? In one sense this is a very old question, as is suggested, for example, by Foucault's attempt to reconstruct ancient ethical or practical thought in terms of "technologies of the self." But Alan Turing gave a new impetus to the question in advancing his theory of what can be computed in a finite number of steps using any method whatsoever. He helped start the picture of the mind as computer program, which would give rise the sort of "cognitive neuroscience" in which today the wiring of our brains comes together with a Darwinism of abilities or skills. Deleuze's image of the relations between thinking and life is of course quite different from such Darwinism of the cognitive; and the difference is shown in the questions of "procedure" and "technique" in the ways thinking is related to life. For him the sense and logic of thinking is not a computational one, and he thus develops a different view of the "machine" of thinking. What he calls "abstract machines" are not Turing machines; they work in different ways and have other relations with our bodies and brains, or what, at one point, he calls "the lived brain." An abstract machine is rather a "diagram of an assemblage" in which computers or computations can of course figure together with us.

Philosophical objections to "strong AI" (the view that the mind just is the computer program of the brain) distinguish the sense of mental operations from their computational simulations; but in working out this sense they often have recourses to more or less phenomenological views about ourselves and our world. Deleuze wants to get beyond such assumptions; in contrast to Gestaltist views, for example, he envisages the brain as operating in an uncertain, indeterminate universe for which Bergson's theory was already suited, where the problem was not one of consciousness but rather of what the brain must be for the kind of "duration" to be possible that breaks with empirical succession of time and psychological memory.[33] But Bergson's ideas were worked out in relation to the "sense" of mechanical and mechanistic "automatisms" rather than informational ones, and so the question arises: can we do for "the cognitive" what Bergson did for "the mechanical" when he proposed a view of the brain no longer subordinated to the reflex-arc, capable of introducing in the interval between stimulus and response a kind of seeing for which there is no "automatic" response? Can we do for digital devices what Man Ray, Jarry, and Tinguely did for mechanical ones, when they invented strange procedures to expose a sense of time and space prior to mechanized operations?[34] We thus approach the question of "abstract machines."

The question is already to be found with the problem of mechanism and mind in classical philosophy—in Descartes's view of "thoughts" and their relation to the body viewed as a kind of automaton, as well as in La Métherie. In Leibniz and Spinoza, Deleuze finds an alternative to Descartes, which in effect views mind and body as both "expressions" of something in life prior to the definition of each—indeed something prior to the nature-artifice distinction. Thus, in what has come to be called Spinoza's "parallelism," he finds his logic of the prepredicative *and*—the logic of a "practical philosophy" of the mind *and* the body, in which the mind goes together "with" the body rather than standing "above" it, giving and receiving orders, as with a Cartesian will.[35] The problem of the "spiritual automaton" then becomes how to deal with the "singular essence" we thus each express in mind as in body as a peculiar *conatus* or desire. That, then, is the kind of question Deleuze later tries to develop in adopting Guattari's talk of "desiring

machines"—machines that "express life" through "constructions," through the connections or syntheses of Deleuze's "logic
of sense." Desiring machines are thus not mechanisms, and are
not to be understood in analogy with mechanisms or mechanical "automatisms." They "cut and connect" with another logic
and sense, and work by breaking down or going awry, and then
starting up again. But if the "desiring machines" that we are
each and together are thus not (and not like) mechanisms, neither are they like a genetically given cognitive program of
testable skills, honed by the survival of the fittest. A desiring
machine is not a Turing machine, and in effect we need to turn
Turing's question around, and ask how Turing machines figure
in the workings of desiring machines, or in the larger, looser assemblages they construct. Deleuze approaches something like
this question in the last pages of his study of cinema, where he
talks of a replacement of nature by information in the images
and signs of modern societies. The problems of "movement" and
"time" in cinema had worked within a largely "mechanical"
sense (e.g., that of Fritz Lang), the problem of an "informational" one being formulated by Kubrick, Godard, and then
Syberberg. If then we think of cinema itself as a kind of "spiritual automaton" or "pyscho-mechanics," we see that the idea of
a purely logical machine has always been accompanied by corresponding sorts of "psychological automatisms," such as those
analyzed by Pierre Janet. For the idea of mind or of thought fully
ordered by itself or internally makes sense only when its relation
to an "outside" has been eliminated. Thinking is in fact never
"automatic" in this way; on the contrary, it works in fits and
starts, and in relation to unforeseeable "shocks" that shake it up
and oblige it to think in new ways; and it is precisely such workings of thought (and therefore the body and brain) that "time-

images" in cinema show us. If thinking is a "machine," it is then one whose logic is related to an outside as it is expressed in body and brain; and the problem is then how to reinvent its operations a world that tends to substitute information for nature. For a whole new kind of training of the mind (and in particular, the eye) goes with this new arrangement, leading to a kind of informational or communicational "stupidity," which thought must combat, and from which it must escape. For thinking is always directed against powers that restrict or block its ramifications and complications. It always deals with powers of another sort— with *potentia* rather than *potestas,* with *puissances* rather than *pouvoirs.*

8

Frege had a logic of the "laws of thought." By contrast, Deleuze may be said to have sought a logic of what, in relation to Spinoza, he calls the powers—the *puissances*—of thought. Such powers are peculiar things. For one thing, they involve something like what Blanchot called an *impouvoir*—an "incapacity" required by thinking and which thinking never completely overcomes. To attain the "powers of thought" is thus to lose one's philosophical self-assurance or bearing through encounter with something that shakes up thought, complicates it, recasts it rules. The humor of the "impossible" in Kafka, for example, would have this function, quite different from the kind of radical freedom of the assertion-stroke in Frege, after which all becomes logically necessary. Deleuze talks of another experience, another conception of the possible, the impossible, and the necessary in his logic. *Puissances* have a different logic than *pouvoirs*—a different "modality" or "temporality."

Deleuze thinks Aristotle tended to enclose the idea of power, as it were, within a logic of the "laws of thought." *Dynamis* was linked to *energeia, potentia* to *actualis,* within his larger categorical scheme or metaphysic, eventually raising difficulties for the attempts to incorporate it within a Christian theology of creation from nothing. Deleuze prefers Whitehead's cosmology of a "creativity" that would precede such categories or the laws made on their basis, capable of generating novelty; and this idea affords him a perspective on Leibniz's theodicy. He is drawn to the problem of future contingents in Aristotle and the new use Leibniz would make of it; in this way we start to see the inflection of a notion of "power" toward that of the "virtuality," which Deleuze will take from Bergon and find in Proust. It is thus through a change in the conception of time or temporality that the idea of "potentia" escapes from the hylemorphic scheme, passing in between the net of species and genera, and discovering strange becomings, whose actualization is freed from all finality. In the place of Leibniz's pyramid of possible worlds, we then have something more like Borges' labyrinth of ever bifurcating paths. Leibniz thought the best world to be "harmonious," allowing for the maximum variety for the simplest laws. But we must see this harmony in terms of the possibility of a "dissonance" that brings together differences—many cities and always another city in the city, as Deleuze puts it at one point.[36] It is only then that we see the full force of Leibniz's principle that the best world is the one with the greatest virtuality; only then are we able to free the idea from its lingering Baroque salvationism (shown in Leibniz through the problem of the saved and the damned), and make it a "pragmatic" matter of experiment and invention. As the idea of "powers" frees itself from the realization of Aristotelian-like categories or laws and becomes a matter of a multiple or complex time or temporality, irreducible to any already given "movement" in time, it acquires a new relation with thought—with the logic and activity of thought; it becomes a matter of what Deleuze calls "the time that takes thought." In place of the problem of the laws of thought, we find one as that of the *affirmation* of powers of thought, powers in thought. For to "affirm life" is never to affirm a proposition or thesis about life, but on the contrary, to engage in another nonassertional style of thinking—to affirm is then to disburden or "lighten," to attain the "innocence" of other possibilities.

Deleuze's logic is thus not a logic of "justified belief" or "warranted assertability." It is more, as with James, a matter of pushing the question of belief beyond the assurance of knowledge, or of faith, to what Deleuze calls a "belief in the world." The problem is already raised in Hume's attempt not only to substitute probable belief for Cartesian certainty, but also to connect it to a sense of self and world prior to religion. For in this way Hume would point ahead to the problem of "empiricist conversion" that Deleuze finds in Kierkegaard (for Protestantism) and Péguy (for Catholicism), when along with Pascal, they substitute for the question of believing in God, that of the modes of existence of the believer and the nonbeliever.[37] For the question of belief is not in the first instance a question of asserting and denying propositions, or even of the legitimacy with which one does so. As the "fiduciary" language used for belief suggests, it is a matter of "credit" or "trust." In this sense, for example, Deleuze says what is interesting in American pragmatism is the attempt to introduce a problem of "trust and truth" no longer subject to any salvationism; thus, in the image of thought, it would substitute for the figure of a judge that of an experimenter who starts to move in a world and in relation to a self that are never given or "conditioned" but are rather in the making.[38] What then does it mean to "credit" or "trust" the world without knowledge or faith, prior to doctrine or propositions "held" as true? One way to see it is in terms of its negative, or what it means to lose such trust. We then find that the world and ourselves appear as "counterfeit" in ways Deleuze finds dramatized not only by Nietzsche, but also by the proto-pragmatist Herman Melville in fiction or Orson Welles in cinema.[39] "Nihilism" is the name Nietzsche gives to this state, in terms of which the question of "affirmation" or of saying "yes" would be directed. Affirmation, in other words, requires a belief or trust in the world and what may yet transpire in it, beyond what we are "warranted" to assert. In *Difference and Repetition,* Deleuze puts the problem in terms of an original relation to the future—of a "belief of the future, in the future."[40] It is a matter of introducing into our view of ourselves and our world this sense of what is to come—of the untimely rather than of the eternal or the transient; it is a matter of rescuing this time—or belief in this time—from mystical or religious thought, as still with Péguy or Kierkegaard, and making it instead at once "worldly" or experimental. Such then is the point where Deleuze's logic of multiplicity becomes inseparable from an affirmation of life.

5: *Life*

1

Multiplicity is not simply a logical, but also a practical matter, a pragmatic matter—something we must make or do, and learn by doing: *"Le multiple, il faut le faire,"* declare Deleuze and Guattari at the start of their *A Thousand Plateaus.*[1] There is a "pragmatics" of the *sens* for which Deleuze proposed a logic quite different from that of the usual study of indexicals, performatives, and presuppositions—the politics of "minor languages" like Black English offers a better example of it. For pragmatics emerges as an original dimension of language just when the element of *sens* is freed from public *Sinn*—to invent a "minor language," for example, one must get away from the notions of public and private that are rooted in "majoritarian" models of standard speech. In linguistics, by contrast, pragmatics remains caught in a standardized syntax or structure or logic—a matter of the "performance" of a "competence" supplied to our brains by our genes.[2] The question posed by the "pragmatics of the multiple" is rather what our brains must be if they can always be remade to enable us to speak in new, nonstandard ways.

The pragmatics of "minor languages" belongs to a larger "practical philosophy" in Deleuze. For the multiplicities we are to make preexist us as individuals as well as given social groups; they are prior to the "molar" ways a society divides us up, to our very ideas of "persons" or "subjects." The idea of multiplicity (and the time of its actualization or invention), in other words, must be introduced into our very conceptions of ourselves, our world, and the different "peoples" we make up—only then do we see its full force as a "practical problem." To think in terms of multiplicities rather than identities—to make or construct multiplicities—requires us to rethink a range of practical concepts of person, action, and belief. Only then can we understand the basic principles in Deleuze's practical philosophy surrounding those problematizing moments that require thinking and in which thinking intervenes—the peculiar time of those questions for which there preexists no automatic or habitual response, no ready program or project, not even an accepted language or description and judgment, which we must experiment and experiment with ourselves to see. Only then do we see the practical problem of making visible and thinkable what is "unattributable" and new in what is happening—and so what has happened or might yet happen—to us. For in Deleuze as with Spinoza a problem in logic ("what is a multiplicity?") becomes a "practical" problem of life ("how to make a multiplicity")—and therefore, a political problem, a problem of "the city."³

To think of ourselves and one another as "multiple," or as "composed of multiplicities," is not to imagine that we have many distinct identities or selves (personalities, brain modules, etc.). On the contrary, it is to get away from understanding ourselves in terms of identity and identification or as distinct persons or selves, however many or "dissociated." It means that we never wholly divide up into any "pure" species, races, even genders—that our lives in fact can never be reduced to the "individualization" of any such pure class or type. Before we are fit into distinct species or strata or classes, we thus compose a kind of indefinite mass or "multitude,"⁴ just as before "major" standards or models of identification or recognition, we each have our "minorities," our "becomings." Multiplicity is not diversity, and making it requires another conception of Life—it is rather as if, under the "second nature" of our persons and identities, there lay a prior potential Life capable of bringing us together without abolishing what makes us singular. Thus Deleuze admires Gabriel Tarde, sociologist of "preindividual" differences in contrast to the "total social fact" in Durkheim and the "anomie" of not belonging to it, or the manner in which Elias Canetti opposed a notion of "packs" to "crowds" and "mass psychology."[5] More generally with the notion of multiplicity he wants to get away from a sociology based on distinctions between individual and society, *Gemeinschaft* and *Gesellschaft*, modernity and tradition, and to pose another kind of question. To form a "pack" rather than a "crowd," to make "differences" where there are only molar or majoritarian identities, to actualize potentials in ourselves as an indefinite multitude—in each case, the problem is to create arrangements (*agencements*) in space and time in which we relate to ourselves and one another in a manner not subordinated to identity or identification, imaginary or symbolic, not even to the self-recognition of classes.

Multiplicity thus leads Deleuze to a new political problem, or rather, a new way of posing the problem of "the political." We should judge political regimes (including democratic ones) in terms of the space they allow for "multiplicities" and their "individuations"—for the time of "a life." But to do this we need to rethink the space and time of politics in terms other than those of a prior or future republic or of an original contract—"another politics, another individuation, another time."[6] Thus in *Cinema 2* Deleuze describes the process through which the problem of the movement of the masses to self-consciousness in a Party is replaced by that of the spaces and times of minorities who can no longer be "represented" by intellectuals—it is rather the intellectuals themselves who must transform themselves as part of such becomings.[7] With this new problem follow new ways of mapping space and time in the postwar European city, as earlier, for example, with geographies drawn by "minor literature" in Kafka's Prague.[8] More generally, Deleuze contrasts "the city" with "the state" in the traditional idea of the political, as if the problem of multiplicity and its time were fundamentally an urban matter—a matter of brains and cities.[9] Thus the great industrial art, the cinema, helps Deleuze to take Nietzsche's "gay science" away from Alpine landscapes as well as from the Black Forest of Heideggerian antiurbanism, and turn instead into an art of the city, its artifice and its "modernity."[10] Already in Proust from out of the stratifications or segmentarities of nineteenth century Paris, we see the emergence of the "complicated time" of a people-to-come, prior even to the "gross statistical categories" of sex and gender.[11] For the "lines" of which our lives are composed are always more complicated and more free than the more or less rigid "segmentations" into which a society tries to sort them, and so they may be used to draw or "diagram" other spaces, other times of living.

2   The problem of "making multiplicities" or "constructing multiplicities" is therefore a problem of life—of "a life," as Deleuze puts it, an indefinite life.[12] But such a life is not to be confused with "the life" of the corresponding individual. It is a potential or virtuality that exceeds the our specification as particular individuals; and we are thus never fully "constituted" or "accomplished" individuals, and our relations with one another may yet pass out through the segments into which our lives are divided up. Such for Deleuze is the force of the "problem of subjectivity" formulated by Hume—our selves or "identities" are never given, indeed our very idea of "the self" is a kind a philosophical fiction.

Our relation to multiplicities and to the time of their actualization is therefore of a very different sort than the connection between memory and "personal identity" through which Locke tried to define "consciousness."[13] Indeed the problem of "time-images" in *Cinema 2* is to show how multiplicities figure in our lives just when their time is freed at once from psychological memory and linear causality, and so from "consciousness." Thus we stand—or "move"—in relation to multiplicities in very different ways than we do to conscious identities or identifications. Although they take us from our "selves" or "persons," in another sense they are what are most peculiar to us or about us. For "a life" is always singular. It is made up of "singularities" that are "preindividual" or "subindividual," which are then linked to others in a plan or "plane" that is impersonal, like the "it" in "it's raining," which is the condition of the singularity of a life. Multiplicities always precede us as constituted selves or conscious persons, and yet it is precisely they and their other possibilities we express to one another as other or *autrui*[14]—thus, for example, we always need "interceders" to open up new paths or sketch new lines in our lives.[15] Our lives must be indefinite or vague enough to include such potential for other worlds of predications or individualizations, and so enter into complications with others that are never fully "explicated." The vagueness of "a life" is thus not a deficiency to be corrected, but rather a resource or reserve of other possibilities, our connections. Indeed it is just because it is vague or unspecified that "a life" is potentially what is most peculiar or singular about us—what makes of us, in Spinoza's terms, "singular essences." What is "peculiar to us" without being "particular about us" is then nothing personal or conscious, but on the contrary, something unattributable, unpredictable in our being and being together.

It is in this way, for example, that taking up the term from Duns Scotus, Deleuze talks of "haeccities." "Haeccities" are "individuations" that are not "individualizations"—not the specification or instantiation of anything, like the singular occurrences that Gerard Manly Hopkins called "haeccities" in his poetry. An hour of a day, a river, a climate, a strange moment during a concert can be like this—not one of a kind, but the individuation of something that belongs to no kind, but which, though perfectly individuated, yet retains an indefiniteness, as though pointing to something "ineffable." A life is in fact composed of many such moments—that is part of what makes it singular. They are the sort of occurrences that come to us rather like the "waves" of which Virginia Woolf spoke—bits of experience that can't be fit into a nice narrative unity, and so must be combined or put together in another way. That the kind of open synthesis or "And" that combines them is irreducible to the "Is" or attributes and identifications is shown precisely in the way time-images in cinema allow for spaces of interrelation that are prior to psychological memory or linear causality, or again in the kinds of "blocks of sensation" in painting that precede distinct figures or narratives. Such occurrences and the waves or blocks through which they are presented in our lives are thus "impersonal." They precede us as subjects or persons, and yet they are always "expressed" in our lives. Even a death should be thought of as singular in this way, as involving an "impersonality" that no "generality" can cover—a sort of "it is dying." Thus Deleuze draws attention to Foucault's discussion of the consequences of Bichat's introduction into the medical conception of death the idea of a singular style;[16] and he proposes to see in Stoic "indifference" to death something akin to Blanchot's "neutrality," the kind of event to which we should not be unequal.[17] Even in dying the problem is to extract a vital "impersonality" from what we are pleased to think of our "persons" or "selves"—as, for example, in the moment between life and death Deleuze finds in his last writing in a story by Dickens.[18]

To get at the "splendid impersonality" of the singularities that precede us as conscious persons requires a peculiar logic of grammar of description, not given through public indexicals or the usual "persons" of discourse, which Deleuze linkens to the tense Lawrence Ferlinghetti called "the fourth person singular," which no one speaks, and of which no one speaks, but which nevertheless subsists in all that is said. It is this strange tense that Deleuze then proposes to see in what Foucault called the "anonymity" of discourse, or the "*on dit*" of *les choses dites*—the "it is talking" or "it is saying" or an "anonymous murmur," which comes before the regularities or procedures that introduce into discourse subject positions, recognizable objects, possible truth-values, and exposes what can be said to "events" that neither logic nor linguistics nor speech-act theory can ever reduce. To attain this unpersonalized murmur is not always easy; it requires the kind of "depersonalizing" or "desubjectivizing" philosophical exercise that, in his last writings, Foucault came to call a "*déprise de soi*" (a withdrawal from oneself).[19] In such cases, impersonality is not an alienation or an "inauthenticity" of *das Man,* but on the contrary the condition of singularization, a lightening-up of life and its possibilities. It is not a generality that abolishes differences but, on the contrary, a condition that frees difference from the determinations of habit, memory, routine, and the practices of recognition or identification within which we are caught, opening up other vital possibilities.

We see this in particular in the way Deleuze approaches the problem of the banal, the routine, the mechanically repro-

ducible in modern art—in Warhol, Beckett, Robbe-Grillet.[20]
To such banality he opposes not the uniqueness of a pure or "auratic" object, but rather a kind of "impersonality" with another
logic, shown, for example, in the small differences Warhol introduced into his series of standard or commercial images. The
problem becomes one of "singularizing" standardized environ-
ments in this manner, introducing into them a variability for
which there exist no "invariants" or standard models—through
"continuous" rather than "discrete" variation in the mathematical language Deleuze adopts. In this way Deleuze proposes to
push the discussion of chance and "automatisms" beyond surrealist devices toward a distinction between chance and probability—he counts dropping a pin on a canvas, for example,
as a matter of probability, not chance.[21] It is precisely such
chance (rather than probability) that characterizes "a life."
Thus Deleuze distinguishes between the "average" or "normal"
person and an indefinite one, a kind of "anybody"—the first is
a statistical entity, the second a vital potential. Foucault had
undertaken a study of the larger "biopolitical" formation, in
which the idea of the statistical norm arose along with many of
the categories through which we would come to describe ourselves, turning, for example, the average adult white heterosex-
ual male into a normal or "majoritarian" identity, the deviations
from which could be analyzed as "abnormalities." In contrast
to such "abnormalities," Deleuze then speaks of "anomalies,"
which instead express forces peculiar to a life or to an "anybody."
Anomalies, he says, are the "edges" of an individuation; to diagram the lines of individuations is then to draw a "plane of life"
that includes the chance of anomalies rather than the probability of deviations from a norm.[22] Deleuze thinks that in
anything worth calling "literature" there is an attempt to

express impersonal "individuations" tracing the ways they figure in our lives, and in a late essay he declares that "literature is posed . . . only by finding under apparent persons the power of an impersonal, which is not a generality but a singularity of the highest degree: a man, a woman, an animal, a stomach, a child. . . ."[23] We might even think of Adam in the Garden of Eden as "vague" in this manner that allows for the chance of "individuations" or as an "anybody" rather than a "first man"—as Deleuze thinks Leibniz started to imagine in passages that, had he developed them, might have freed his idea of "compossibility" from the harmonious "perfectionism" and the lingering salvationism in which it was still enclosed.[24]

3   The unconscious is "impersonal" in just this "splendid" way. It is made up of multiplicities that precede us as conscious persons, requiring a "pragmatics," or *agencement* not based in personal pronouns like "I" or "we." "What an error to have ever said '*the* id'!" Deleuze and Gauttari exclaim on the first page of their first book, *The Anti-Oedipus*—better to talk of distributions of energy "here and there" (*ça et là*). In *Difference and Repetition,* Deleuze had tried to push the Freudian conception of the unconscious in this direction, connecting it to his idea of "series" and their "virtualities." For example, he wrote of the "part-objects" of the libidinal body as "foyers of virtuality," which would trace strange paths in the fabric of a life—something that we would thus "live" through, a complicating repetition irreducible to conscious memory.[25] Such foyers of bodily "virtuality" would be linked to others in an "informal plane" of life, prior and irreducible to a "symbolic order" and our "imaginary" relations to it. The practical problem

of "a life" might then be said to be how to attain such libidinal virtualities, and put them first, bringing them together in ways that would precede our identifications with a given social or cultural order. In his essay on totemism, Lévi-Strauss had advanced the "structuralist" idea that what falls outside such an order acquires the sense of sacrifice and transgression. But Deleuze wanted a positive or pragmatic rather than a negative or sacrificial picture of what is thus "outside" a social order; he wanted to understand "the outside" in terms of the virtuality of other possible relations, or in terms of impersonal individuations that couldn't simply be derived from a father's "no." Thus repression would not come first, but would rather be understood in terms of a vital power that "repeats" the events of such individuations, in the "rhythms" through which they are played out in our lives. We don't repeat because we repress, Deleuze wrote in *Difference and Repetition;* more fundamentally, we repress or "forget" in order to live our desires in this other unpersonalized manner, which makes of our lives each singular "complexes" of desire. As with Spinoza's "practical philosophy" of desire, the question then becomes how to construct a "plane of compositions" in which our "singular essences" might be "composed" with one another, while yet remaining singular.

To say we each have "a life" and to say that we each have *an* unconscious thus amounts to the same thing. It means that there is always something outside our "identifications" as subject or persons, which we play out through complexifying encounters—as, for example, with the "series of lovers" in Proust. The whole question of "sexuation" needs be understood in this way, rather than through Oedipal identification; underneath the "gross statistical categories" of sex and gender lie a whole "molecular" multiplication of our peculiarities, which then come out in strange ways and times, giving rise to highly original "compositions" or "virtualities." Thus, for example, Deleuze talks of a "becoming-woman" that everyone, even women, must go through in departing from normal or "majoritarian" models of what is to be a man or a woman.[26] For reasons of strategy or simple survival, it sometimes becomes necessary in the process of such "becomings" to say one is finally discovering the true "identity" of being a woman. But the logic of the becoming always goes beyond such assertions of rediscovered identity. For a becoming is never a "history" with fixed starting and ending points. Rather, itself the imitation or representation of nothing, it shifts and complicates the very terms of identification.

The problem with psychoanalysis is that having discovered such presubjective "powers," such complicating impersonal "virtualities" of our libidinal bodies and their "vicissitudes" in our lives, it enclosed them with a new system of "personalizing" identification—that of the family and the "images" of familial persons, as if the unconscious were only a kind of deficient identification within the familial order. When, for example, "a life" is shown in literature, a psychoanalytically inspired criticism is there to bring it all back to the "family romance" of the characters, if not of the author. For Deleuze such "familialism" explains nothing; on the contrary, it is just what needs to be explained. He thinks it arose in reaction to what amounts to a kind of "decoding" or "deterritorialization" of the hold of the family on the unconscious "complexes" of desire in our lives. Early on, Jacques Lacan said that Freud's discovery of the Oedipus complex came precisely at a time of a dissolution of the actual authority of fathers. In effect it was a way of analyzing the resulting problems or maladies of desire by postulating a "symbolic" Father—a kind of mythical Urvater without whom it would not be possible to maintain one's sense of self or "sexual identity." Deleuze wanted to go further, pushing the idea of unconscious entanglements of desire beyond this great master complex supposed to "overcode" or "reterritorialize" all the others. We should understand our identifications with a social order in terms of the roles they assume within the unfolding of our singular, indefinite lives rather than trying to reinsert the complicated lines of those lives back into a master law of our relations to the "symbolic order." Thus we need another picture of unconscious desire itself and the kind of "complex" it forms that is no longer "transgressive" or "sacrificial"; we should rather see it a "constructivist" manner in terms of this informal plane through which our libidinal virtualities are played out. We might then read Freud's great diagnoses of the pathologies of paternity in another way or from another angle—we might see them in terms of nonidentificatory ways of composing or arranging what is singular in our desires, in terms of the construction of "planes of composition" for ourselves as singular complexes of desire, or as "multiple" erotic bodies. The practical problem of unconscious desire would then be that of inventing an eros and an erotics freed from mimesis—impersonal yet singularizing— that takes us from our "selves" or "egos" yet without "fusing" us together, closer to Ovid's metamorphoses than the steadfastness of Aristotelian friends.

Multiplicities are unconscious, then, because their individuations are impersonal; and conversely, what makes desire unconscious is not some "primal repression" but rather the unfolding of events and powers in life that can't be contained within personalizing identifications, and work themselves out through other "multiplying" or "complexifying" kinds of encounter and interaction. By thus introducing multiplicity into eros, Deleuze tries to get away from the traditional role of *mimesis* in *paidea*— from the centrality of the ideas of identity and identification in our conception of our formation or "civilization." The question then becomes how to conceive of our ethos—our "modes of being"—in a manner no longer based in identity.

4   We must see ourselves as Leibnizian "vague Adams" or as Spinozistic "singular essences" or as each having *an* unconscious—a singularizing indefinite unconscious. Deleuze finds a related problem in the modern novel with the theme of "being without qualities"—or, as Deleuze puts it at one point, of becoming so "smooth" that no qualities stick to one, like those "on the road" in American literature.[27] The emergences of such "unqualifiable" figures, and their manner of "filling out" (*remplir*) space and time, alter the shape of the novel. The time of what happens and what has happened frees itself from the more "rationalized" or "neurotic" plot of the European novel, and discovers the sort of "heterogeneity" Bakhtin would see in the Russian novel as well as the movement and looseness or formlessness Deleuze finds in the American one. Life becomes "indefinite" in the novel just when characters cease to be completed or individualized persons, and instead become "originals," brought together in new spaces and times of interrelation. For those "without qualities" are no longer able to tell straight narratives in which to "recognize themselves"; they start to move in another temporality given rather through juxtaposition or superposition of different blocks, which themselves can become undone and mutate. In this situation, complexifying encounter replaces identifying recognition as a basic procedure through which events unfold. Similarly, replac-

ing the "movement" of recognition in classical film narrative, Fellini, for example, would turn encounter in postwar Rome and the urban spaces peculiar into an original cinematic procedure, tied up with the emergence of "other possible worlds."

With the procedure of encounter there goes a particular view of the other, which Deleuze develops in contrast to the model of more or less mutual, more or less happy recognition. Thus he takes issue with Sartre's portrait of "concrete relations with others" as a futile passion, rooted in a desire for an impossible recognition, saying that it preserves the very notion of subject and object from which Sartre's idea of the "transcendence of the ego" ought to have freed him. In a novel of Michel Tournier, he finds a kind of inference from absence to another idea—the idea of *autrui* as the "expression of a possible world." It supposes very different notions of space, vision, and perversion than a Sartrian duel of gazes in a café or the shameful look through a keyhole, closer to encounter and series of lovers in Proustian "erotomania." The notion of encounter as a source of events that "transcend the ego" supplies Deleuze with a way out of the conception of the problem of self and other in the great Hegelian tale of recognition Sartre took from Kojève, as well as the more "structuralist" problematic of a "misrecognition" of one's position in a social order, and allows him to pose another problem: how to express those "immanent" possibilities of a life that "transcend" our identifications or that lie beneath our "gross" personalizations or personalities. That, in effect, is the problem posed by encounter and "unqualifiable" characters in fiction; and it is in turn tied up with a larger question of the possibilities of interrelations that compose a given "society." Sociologists had tended to divide such possibilities by distinguishing between organic "community" and individualistic "society," the first traditional, the second modern. Deleuze formulates another problem, or another way of conceiving of the problem of "modernity"—how to create relations between "originals," who depart from the regime of social recognition with a procedure such as Bartleby's "I would prefer not to" in Melville's short story, how to invent spaces and times in which our "preindividual" and "presocial" singularities might come out and merge with one another. The problem posed by those "anybodies" who can no longer be "qualified" either as individuals or as members of organic wholes is, then, that of a modern ethos, or manner of being, that would allow for a "community" among ourselves as "singular essences," no longer subordinated to the "representation" or "imitation" of anything.

Heidegger thought the problem of "ethos" or dwelling was a more basic or original one than the construction of an "ethics"; and yet he tended to imagine "dwelling" or "inhabiting the Earth" in terms of a historical *Volk* rooted in a place.[28] Deleuze understands "ethos" (and so "ethics") in another way, in terms of "manners of being" or "modes of being" and their distribution in space and time—what at one point he calls "nomos."[29] He talks of a kind of "manner-ism" in ethics, or again, in relation to Spinoza, an original "etho-logy" in the compositions of our singular modes of being.[30] Deleuze's "ethos" thus has a different relation to space and to place than the "being-there" of a people in a site or territory. The problem of "those without qualities," or of "minor languages," for example, is not that of a "majoritarian" land, but involves other notions of proximity and distance, time and history, as suggested, for example, by Kafka's Chinese wall.[31] On the contrary, the problem is to invent a *chez soi,* an "at home" of a very different kind, no longer given in the opposition of "lived place" to "abstract space," and requiring a different idea of what territories and borders are. What would it mean to think of ourselves as "natives" of—as "being at home" in—this strange space-time that, like the *chora* in Plato's *Timaeus,* comes before the delimitation of territory and the logic of pure types, and the species and genera into which they divide; how then might we see division into identificatory territories?[32] That is the problem about "ethos" that Deleuze tries to get at not only in talking about "deterritorialization," but also an original idea of "the Earth" and the sort of "people" who inhabit or are the natives of it. For "the Earth" that is supposed in thinking of ourselves as singular modes of being is not localizing and identifying, but on the contrary, something formless, uncentered, subsisting within the borders of our "territorializations." To make it the source of an "ethos," to learn to be "at home" in it, then, is to see oneself as native of it prior to the identifying territories of family, clan, or nation, and so to see oneself as a kind of stranger to the "self" given by such identifications. It is to learn to be at home rather in "a life"—in one's splendidly impersonal" unconscious—developing a sort of savoir faire with it.

A life or an unconscious, then, supposes a view of territories and movement that might be put in these terms: there is no establishment or delimitation of a territory that does not carry with it a potential for "deterritorialization," and the deterritorialization may become "absolute" when there is no way back from it and no known territory to which it will lead. "Minor languages" like Black English pose this problem—one must devise ways of being at home not in a territory but in this Earth, which, far from rooting them in a place, an identity, a memory, releases them from such borders and becomes light or deterritorialized, like a tent put down by nomads, or the topographies drawn by the vital rhythms of the dance invoked by Zarathustra when he tells of how the Earth becomes light.[33] The problem is no longer that of "the people," but of "a people," an indefinite people, as yet "without qualities," still to be invented, of the sort to which Deleuze thinks Kafka was led when he declared, "It is impossible to write in Czech, in Yiddish, or in German, and yet impossible *not* to write"—a sense of impossibility shown in his invention of a kind of "foreign language" in official German, as yet spoken by no one group. What Deleuze terms minority always supposes such a "people to come," born of an "absolute deterritorialization," even if, for reasons of strategy or sheer survival, it is necessary to "compensate" it with a counteridentity or counternation, as in what he calls "relative deterritorialization." We must understand such relative or strategic counterterritories, in other words, in terms of a light or deterritorialized Earth that precedes them, posing the question of ethos or dwelling in terms of it.

Deleuze's "deterritorialized" mannerism or ethos thus involves an ethics not of purity and piety in identification, but rather of a complexity and a dignity in our manners of being, which precede "pure" identification or imitation. The problem of dignity is basic to the sense Deleuze tries to give to "ethics," and the way it contrasts with "moralities" of obedience to established values; the basic question, which Deleuze finds in Stoicism and then makes his own, is "not to be unworthy (*indigne*) of what happens to us"—in particular, how to respond to those individuations that precede us as subjects and persons, that make up a life. Such, for example, would be the "democratic dignity" exemplified by Bartleby's "I would prefer not to," in the New York of a proto-pragmatist America. But the question is also to be found in various forms throughout modern literature, and in the time and space peculiar to it; and in the plateau in *A Thou-sand Plateaus,* devoted to question of being *chez soi* in a "deter-ritorialized" or "light" Earth, Deleuze tries to redraw the map of artistic movements accordingly.[34] Classicism lacks the con-cepts of "people" and "territory" that Romanticism would in-troduce in terms of roots and identity; but in modernism a new kind of problem arises—that of the spaces that might bring to-gether our "singularities" to form a "people to come," foreign or minor in all established places or languages, which would make us "natives" of geographies the maps of which precede and re-draw the borders of established territories. In the modern work, we thus find the problem of "making a multiplicity"—the at-tempt to create uncentered spaces prior to personalized identi-ties and identifications, and so to invent new "habits of saying I and we" no longer tied down to identification or representa-tion, which might thus spare us from what, in a conversation with Foucault, Deleuze called the "indignity of speaking for others."[35]

5

We thus always each have "a life" prior and irre-ducible to the gross identifications that attach us to familial, social, national, or sexual territories; the problem is how to attain it, what to do with it. In part it is a question of history—indeed one may say that as Deleuze uses the terms, whereas majorities have history, only minorities have "becomings." It is precisely the historically indefinite or "unqualifiable" nature of a life that allows for processes in which we depart from our given or constituted selves without knowing in advance quite who or what we may become—what Deleuze calls "becoming-other." All real becoming is such "becoming-other" and so contrasts with the imitation of anything prior as well as with stories with fixed beginnings or ends. Deleuze thinks that at all times or in all histories there is at least a potential for becoming—we all have our "minorities," we each have *an* unconscious. One consequence is that a given society or culture is never exhausted by its constitutive relations or distinctive divisions; on the contrary, it is always "leaking" (*en fuite*), and may be analyzed or "diagrammed" in terms of its "lines of flight" (*lignes de fuite*). No society, in other words, can rule out completely the possibility of what Foucault came to call "processes of subjectivization" that would take us from our "constituted" selves to "other spaces"— for example, those "movements" that Foucault thought were taking us away from the whole idea of "sexuality" found in the normalizing psychiatry of the last century so as to become something other, though we were not yet quite sure who or what. Underneath its gross divisions and unities a society is thus always "complicated" or "complex" in ways not contained in its more recognized conflicts or contradictions, giving rise to the questions Foucault called "problematizations," for which there preexists no consensus, no "we think." That is the sort of question raised by "molecular" differences subsisting within larger "molar" social divisions and conflicts, or shown in a kind of "micropolitics." The existence of "lines of flight," in other words, requires that we rethink our picture of "social space"—or our idea that space is in itself social—so as to make room for the microdynamics of a life that no more resides in a place than it is caught up in an alienating "abstract space." We need a mapping and an "ethology" of another kind. Deleuze thinks we already find something like it in the Leibnizian "preindividual differences" Gabriel Tarde tried to introduce into social space—as it were, spaces of "anybody" rather than the normal or statistical man as the spaces of "a life." The great question of the "banalization" of space in modern societies might then be attacked not by unique or auratic objects nor by properly "contextualized" or "grounded" ones, but rather through strategies of singularization that would lighten spaces, releasing vital differences in them. But what sort of "geometry" must we then attribute to social space—to the "sociality" or "sociability" of space?

To get at precisely such questions, Deleuze introduces a conception of the "segmentations" of life with which "making multiplicities" would always have to contend.[36] Societies tend to divide up our lives into more or less rigid segments, and yet there is no *completely* segmented, no fully stratified space. For there is no stratification that does not secrete the possibility of other complicating relations, capable of combining with others in another looser nonsegmented plan allowing for "in-between spaces," disparities, becomings; and we must thus always distinguish between segmented and nonsegmented kinds of multiplicity, even when the two in fact are to be found in the same space. Thus even the hard "disciplinary" segmentations of space and time, whose diagram Foucault drew in modern societies, have their "lines of flight," their "becomings," indeed a whole "micropolitics" that departs from the "normalizing individualization" (and so from the "average man") to invent other vital singular manners of being.[37] If, then, segmentation of social space permits a geometry of horizontals and verticals within which to chart or locate all social "movement," minorities and becomings work instead with "diagonals" or "transversals," which suggest other spaces, other movements. To "diagram" a space is to expose such diagonal lines and the possibilities they open up, making a *carte* that is not a *calque*—a map that is not the "tracing" of anything prior, but which serves instead to indicate "zones of indistinction" from which becomings may arise, if they are not already imperceptibly in the making. In other words, social space can never be fully drawn from "Cartesian coordinates," since it always "envelopes" many "infraspaces" that introduce distances and proximities of another, nonquantifiable sort. In "developing" such potentials we should no longer think in terms of lines going from one fixed point to another, but, on the contrary, must think of points as lying at the intersection of many entangled lines, capable of drawing out "other spaces"—a bit as with one of Jackson Pollock's lines, a line that no longer traces a contour, but is itself always bifurcating into others. The problem then becomes to "make lines" rather than to "make a final point" (*faire le point*).

Such lines and the "other spaces" they draw, then, are what make a society "open" in a sense somewhat different from that of Karl Popper—a sense closer to that of Bergson, who talked about an "open society" before Popper, or to Rossellini's cinematic portrait of Rome as an "open city." To think of societies as Bergsonian "open wholes" is to imagine that beneath their official histories and divisions there exist other powers, actualized through other kinds of encounter and invention—powers of a sort Marx thought tended to flourish precisely as one passes from the country to the city to breathe the vital air of urban "deterritorializations." But where Marx attempted to analyze such powers (and deterritorializations) from the standpoint of different classes and the Parties that "represent" them, Deleuze proposed to see them rather in terms of a picture of "minorities" and "molecular differences," of becomings and "other spaces," which no Party can hope to represent or direct from above. What matter in his larger social "diagrams" are thus the processes of "decoding" and "deterritorialization" that capitalism carries with it in its ever-expanding attempts to interconnect goods and people, labor and money. The connections between financial capital, integrated markets, and electronic media now known as "globalization" are no exception. We are confronted with a new modernization whose map is drawn by the new geographies of poverty or the unequalities of wealth, as well as by the new patterns of immigration that have redistributed the configurations of the great metropolises of an earlier industrial and colonial phase of capitalism. Deleuze thinks even the industrial "proletariat" thrown off in that earlier phase of capitalism, more than a distinct social "stratum" or class, should itself be seen as a kind of unstratified mass "without qualities," whose "processes of subjectivization" would then redraw the map of society, obliging to invent new strategies, even new kinds of legal entity. No Party, no group of intellectuals, can ever fully represent or direct such "movements," such "becomings," such *fuites* of a society, and no *prise de conscience* ever suffices to grasp it—indeed it is precisely the political dilemma of thinking of "open society" in this Bergsonian sense that "we no longer dispose of an image of the proletariat of which it would suffice to take consciousness."[38] Thus the very relation of intellectuals to such "movements" or "processes of subjectivizations" must change, passing from a "representational" to an "experimental" role, freeing the "social imagination" from the representation of anything given, prior, original. Thus they would become part of the "fabulation of a people to come," which, no longer tied down the "imagined communities" of a time or a place, would contrast with the myths of a past or original people—as Deleuze puts it in terms taken from Bergson. Majorities may then have their official histories and memories; there will always be minorities to experiment with those other "peoples" in each and all of us for which history rather supplies only the "negative conditions."

6 There is a problem in experimentation with the spaces of such a multiple nonidentificatory *habitus* or *nomos,* which concerns the violence inherent in "pure" identifications; and indeed dignity in our multiple ethos itself runs the risk of becoming the object of murderous hatred and reprisal. Deleuze discusses the problem of this sort of violence already in his first book on Hume, where it is posed in relation to the "problem of subjectivity" that arises when we no longer take the self as given, but rather as deriving from relations of habit and memory and hence from the "conventions" of a society—as it were, from the habits of saying "I." For it follows that it would be wrong to imagine society as made up of "given" selves, who, as "constituting" subjects, would then confer on the state its legitimacy; we must rather look to the prior questions of how subjects are themselves "constituted" in the first place, or to what Hume calls "conventions." What Deleuze admires is the manner in which Hume was thus able to depart from classical contract theory, and pose instead the problem of the "credibility" of governments.[39] From this "naturalist" (rather than theological) standpoint, Hume was able to pose a new problem—the problem of our "partiality" to the particular groups in which we find ourselves. Left to themselves, our identifications with family, clan, nation, or "community" would lead to terrible violence, and the problem posed by this potential violence is one that cannot simply be settled through a more or less "rational" arrangement of interests or choices—neither *Gemeinschaft* nor *Gesellschaft* can contain it. The problem of "partiality" is thus a problem not of "egoism," to be resolved by a more rational organization of interests, but rather of the passions and the institutions that form them—hence of "artificial virtues" and "civility" in our manners of being. Of course one may object that such "civilized manners" in turn often simply carry the violence of class and class divisions, but this only displaces the problem. The problem is that identity is violent as such—there is a violence (or "barbarity") in our very constitution as "subjects" or "selves," and we must rethink our notions of contract and institution accordingly.

In *A Thousand Plateaus,* Deleuze says more generally that there exists a kind of violence that remains "outside" the state—a violence of forces that no state can control or rationalize in advance, and which often comes to the fore in cities or is worked out through city- rather than state-forms—as, for example, with the questions posed by the *favellas* and *banlieux,* which are the shame of our contemporary cities.[40] Indeed one might say that in Deleuze, a city-state tension tends to replace the great state-society distinction that Foucault came to see as the chief limitation of modern political thought. For what is "outside" the state is not a nice "civil society," but rather all sorts of *fuites,* minorities, becomings that escape states or that they must try to "capture." The problem with the contractual tradition in modern political thought from Hobbes to Hegel is, then, in effect, that it tries to rule out in advance such "violence" in our constitution—in Hobbes by giving violence of the sovereignty of states, in Hegel by "converting" ("sublating" or "sublimating") it into the political forms of the *Rechstaat* through the dialectical work of history.

In Spinoza as well as in Hume, Deleuze discerns another kind of political philosophy—another view of the relation between politics and philosophy—that would rather allow for this "outside" and the sort of questions that come from it. Indeed it is just when the philosopher starts to formulate the problems of this outside that Deleuze thinks he ceases to be a "public professor" like Hobbes, concerned to work out and defend the legitimate form of the State. He then starts to work with a violence that escapes "capture" within such forms—for example, all the forces that today depart from "capture," from the more or less welfarist or socialist rationality of the modern nation-state, of which, in *A Thousand Plateaus,* Deleuze mentions multinational corporations, "ecumenical" religious formations, electronic "global villages," and above all, "minorities," old and new. The violence of such forces is shown in the insistence with which they move into territories and raise questions that don't seem to fit in ways of doing things, or received political philosophies, obliging us to "think in other ways"—it is just that which distinguishes such violence from the kinds that can already be predicted, explained, or controlled by knowledge or by those kinds that can already be fit within accepted forms of judgment and legitimation. For in politics not only is one always in fact obliged to proceed by "experimentation, groping about, injection, retrieval, advance, retreat";[41] there is also no form of government that can rule out or completely silence those problems that are not obstacles to be removed but rather are points around which new "becomings" arise, new ways of thinking take shape.

Thus one might talk about the violence of the "problematizations" that led to the establishment of social rights or the kind of "welfare" for which national states must be responsible, or of the problematization of aristocratic privileges that led to the defense by such states of our civil or human rights, or again of the ones that today, beyond borders of sovereign nation-states, try to pose new ways of understanding and "enforcing" such rights. Such indeed for Foucault was the violence of the problematizations introduced by the forces of 1968, when there arose new questions (surrounding women, minorities, sexuality, work, the environment, etc.) that were "posed to politics without themselves being reinscribed in a political theory"[42]—those questions that show that politics exists just because there is no final theory or science of it.

7   Foucault was to find that "speaking truly and freely" about such problems or such violence was in fact not something a society countenances easily. In an unfinished series of lectures and writings, he asked what it might mean for our understanding of politics itself to introduce the question of a violence in our very constitution, which would be irreducible to the Hobbesian idea of state-sovereignty as well as the Hegelian scheme of the dialectical conversion of violence to the state.[43] Perhaps the whole idea of "sovereignty," he suggested, was still a piece of theology—a modern vestige of what Spinoza had analyzed as the "politico-theological." Thus, in contrast with Carl Schmitt, Foucault disowned the Hobbesian fiction of a "war of all against all" as the origin of the state, and proposed in its place a "strategic" (as distinct from "juridical" or "theological") conception of power, or of politics, as a kind of war carried on within given conditions and in relation to particular problems; he even came to see Bataille's ideas about sovereignty as a kind of "retroversion."[44] Such a conception of politics (or "the political") might thus allow one to get at those questions that come before state-sovereignty and involve a nondialectizable violence in what

actually makes or constitutes us as subjects. What then are the costs and the risks of speaking truly of such violence?[45] For one must deal with a kind of violence that cannot simply be "represented" subjectively or intersubjectively—one that requires other, less direct styles of expression, as well as a manner of "questioning politics" that must create connections and alliances where none previously existed. In asking such questions, Foucault rejoins a problem in Deleuze—a problem that, in a note reversing Foucault's preference for "pleasure" over "desire" in his *History of Sexuality,* Deleuze suggests that he himself had posed in a "masochistic" manner rather than in Foucault's "sadistic" one.[46] One version of the problem is "showing the intolerable," which Deleuze thought Foucault in fact shared with neo-Realism; another, what Primo Levi had called "the shame of being human" (as distinct from guilt and retribution); still another, Francis Bacon's attempt to show "the meat" and so oppose a prefigurative, prenarrative "violence of sensations," illustrating nothing, to the kind of "sensationalized violence" that Bacon had associated with photographic cliché. In such cases we find a relation to violence that is not about mastery or sublimation—a relation that is rather "diagnostic" or "clinical."

It is in his presentation of Masoch that Deleuze elaborates this idea of a "clinical" kind of "critique." Before they became names of diseases eventually to be conflated with one another, he thinks Masoch and Sade were "diagnostic" authors—diagnostic, in particular, of a strange pathology accompanying the kind of "morality" Kant tried to introduce into modern philosophy, or the notion of "civilization" associated with it. In this way, Deleuze takes up a problem posed by Freud, which Jacques Lacan had formulated in his essay "Kant with Sade," also to be found in other forms in Nietzsche or in Kafka—how to have an ethics that would no longer be subordinated to the morality of the superego and its peculiar kind of cruelty or "sadism." Freud, wrote Deleuze, had elaborated the "paradox of conscience"—the greater or more refined one's sense of conscience or its "call," the more guilty one feels. That is what Lacan had called the *"gourmandise"* of the superego—the more you feed it the more it wants.[47] The solution to this paradox in Freud, according to Deleuze, was to see that we don't repress our desires because we have a conscience; rather, in the first place, we have a conscience because we repress (if not "sublimate" or "civilize") our desires. We then see there is a problem of an "ethic of desire" that comes before the morality of conscience or superego. In ancient ethics, we find a tendency to make the Law revolve around Good— Socrates' suicide may be seen as a dramatization of the submission of the justice of the Law to the requirements of the Good of the City. Kant revolutionized this. He proposed to see the Good as revolving around the Law and its "categorical" call for obedience ("act as if . . ."), finding in such obedience the source of a freedom from the "instrumental" world or ends and its "hypothetical" imperatives. Freud's paradox is then a diagnosis of the pathologies of the categorical inner duty, which Kant tried to rationalize as the path to the "realm of ends," or as the source of our freedom. If Sade and Masoch are "diagnostic" (rather than "sick") writers, it is then in part because they expose the "violence" of desire in Kantian-style moralities each from a different angle—Sade in relations to institutions, Masoch in relation to contracts. Erotic "masochism" is of course an age-old phenomenon, but Deleuze thinks Masoch used it to give a humoristic, playful diagnosis—a diagnosis, for example, of the role that the idealized "cold" women plays, like a Venus in furs, within the "masochistic" attitudes or behavior of ethnic minorities. In the same way, the "masochistic" elements in Kafka's violent humor form part of a larger diagnosis of the "diabolical forces knocking at the door."

What then should we make of the diagnosis of such violence in our desires or the kind of pathology it exposes in moralism of the Kantian type? It is here that Deleuze parts company with Freud and Bataille, who, he thinks, preserve too much of the figure of the Priest, diagnosed by Nietzsche as by Spinoza before him. He thinks we need another view of desire itself no longer based in a "primal" repression or transgression—more "constructivist," more "compositional." In Nietzsche, the problem is tied up with the violence (and taste for violence) found in ancient tragedy—one might read Antigone, for example, as a feminine figure who dramatizes this Law that always precedes the particular laws or the good of a city, and what happens when one tries to act upon it. But Deleuze wanted to push the question of violence beyond such "Oedipal" figures of disobedience toward the mystery of the affirmation in Nietzsche's Ariadne.[48] *Hamlet* marks the change—in it we find a new notion of time, which, beyond tragic "cycles" of revenge, might allow for an "affirmation of Life" and the presubjective, presignifying violence that is inseparable from it.

8   Hamlet is a new kind of hero for Deleuze, unlike Oedipus or Antigone; he starts to move in another time—a time freed from a prior Law as well as from a *"physis"* or nature that returns to itself: "the time of the city and nothing else," as Deleuze will call it.[49] It is not a "messianic" time, but more a Baroque one, with its play of masks, shown in the way action, character, and sign or image change in that drama. Classical drama had tended to envisage time in terms of a movement "in which" things occur—in particular, the words and deeds that make up "character." But in literature, as in philosophy, we start to see another view of time that can no longer fit within such a movement. In short stories, for example, Deleuze thinks that the question of what has happened is turned into a kind of secret that is not a hidden content to be revealed as in a detective story, but rather something, expressed more in the "postures" than in the "positions" of bodies, that points obscurely to what might yet take place.[50] It is this other time that is thus "in us," expressed or implicated in our bodies and their modes of being as a kind of force or power, which Deleuze tries to bring out—indeed his *Cinema 2* may be read as a complex study of it and the ways in which it contrasts with the kind of "movement" that had predominated prewar cinema. In philosophy, Deleuze thinks the problem was formulated by Kant when he proposed to think of time as a "form of intuition," preparing the way for philosophers like Bergson or James, who would introduce a kind of indetermination and multiplicity into such time and its intuition, thus anticipating what cinema would work out through its "time-images."[51]

For Deleuze, Hamlet is thus not the hero of doubt or skepticism, but rather the hero of this other time that may take one from one's self or character, and expose one to those points in a history from which other unforeseen points emerge. He is the one to declare "the time is out of joint"—out of the "joints" of any prior movement, cyclical or linear; he is the one who must move in this other time that neither "comes back" nor "goes forward," but is constantly deviating from its course. It is this time and its intuition that remove the whole problem of agency, action, and character away from an original nature or contract to which things might come back, and makes it rather a matter of this "time of the city" that, no longer tied down to natural cycles or obedient to divine laws, would be expressed rather through the play of a superior artifice. When Plato introduced the question of time into the concept of city or *polis* (hence of "citizen" and the "civic"), it came with his poisoned gift of transcendence. He imagined a pure, perfect timeless *polis*-idea or *polis*-plan we had forgotten we had already seen in a preexistence, but which, in this imperfect, unjust, and transient world, we must learn to imitate in our souls. In other words, he subordinated the time of the city to mimesis of pure forms that remained the same in their more or less adequate effectuations or instantiations; even though the whole question is in fact to associate time with another kind of "plan," no longer given through the link between form and matter.

When the question of time was then reintroduced within the theological context of the man-city of God, Plato's poison would remain, and it is perhaps in Giordono Bruno or in Plotinus that we find a deviation more congenial to Deleuze. He thinks that Spinoza along with a Baroque Leibniz depart from the Platonic plan to discover time as a complicating force in a material rather than as a form imposed on matter. Thus Leibniz would introduce the problem of "compossibility" into the idea of the city or the time of the city; and Spinoza would perhaps go further, when he proposed to think of the "point of view" of eternity outside the theologico-political tradition as the point of view of singularity and its composition—indeed it was just in this say that he could depart from Descartes's notion of agency or will as a mental event that precedes and causes actions, and pose the problem of freedom instead in "expressivist" or "constructivist" terms.

The secret of the notion of eternal return in Nietzsche is then for Deleuze to take up this thread again, posing it in terms of a time that is neither eternal nor transient, but rather "untimely." For the eternal return is in fact not the thought that everything might come back the same, but rather that difference is always coming back and must be affirmed again in each case as such— it is in this way that the thought becomes "selective." Deleuze thinks only this differentiating or singularizing time that precedes us, and that exposes us to another logic of individuation and invention, is capable of freeing us from an "original" nature, contract, or law we must imitate or obey, and so allows us to really experiment with ourselves. The affirmation of "a life," in other words, requires the affirmation of this time, which appears in Hamlet as "the time of the city and nothing else." To affirm ourselves—to construct and express ourselves—as multiple, complicated beings brought together before any transcendent model or plan, in other words, we require a time not of Chronos but of Aion.[52] Nietzsche's secret then becomes that of his Ariadne, heroine of affirmation rather than of guilt and law, who, hanging herself with the thread her father gave her, abandoned by the mythic hero of Athenian democracy, is freed to turn to an affirmative dance and "engagement" with the light-footed Dionysus.

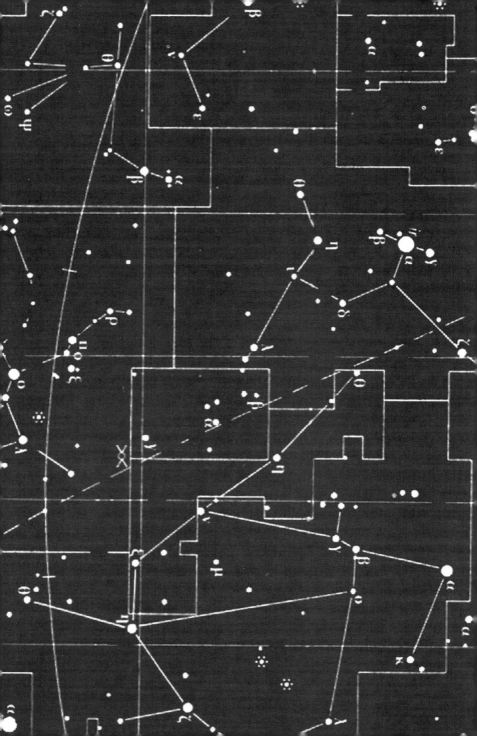

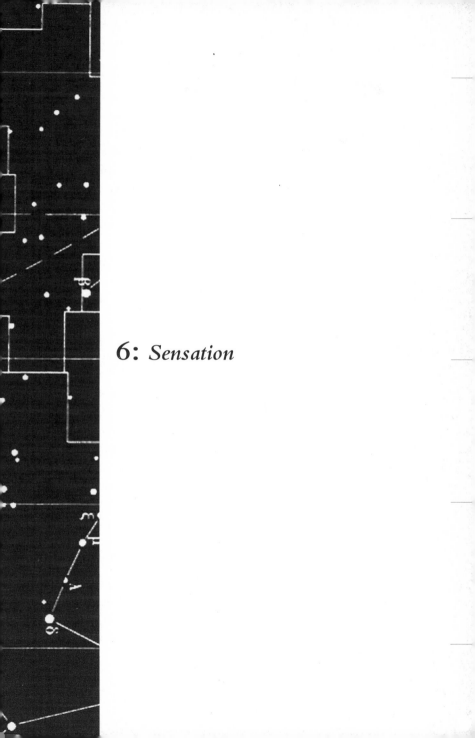

6: *Sensation*

1   The relation of philosophy to art is a delicate one, fraught since Plato with a strange rivalry and identification. Deleuze's view of the relation is more Nietzschean than Kantian. His aesthetic takes the form not of a judgment, but rather of an experimentation and creation that defies judgment. Of Kant, he says that he never really made a *critique* of judgment; and he demands "what expert judgment, in art, could bear on the work to come?"[1] But although it does not judge, Deleuze's philosophy nevertheless "selects" from the arts and from what we are inclined to call "art." "Among all those who make books with literary intentions," he declares, "very few can call themselves writers";[2] similarly, he sees the history of cinema as a "long martyrology."[3] "Perhaps therein lies the secret," he confides in a late essay, "to make exist, not to judge."[4]

The relation between philosophy and art is nevertheless an intrinsic one for Deleuze. He thinks that a nonphilosophical understanding of philosophy is at work in and through the arts, and that philosophy always presupposes such an understanding, and, indeed, is in part addressed to it. Many writers or artists have "understood" Spinoza in this way, for example—they have invented a kind of "Spinozism" within their work, which in turn helps to concretize the difference in Spinoza between a "plane of immanence" and a "plan of organization."[5] To formulate the problems and to work out the concepts in such nonphilosophical understandings, on the other hand, is itself a philosophical activity. Thus, in "producing the concepts" that are "given" in cinema (as distinct from applying ready-made concepts to it), Deleuze considers himself to be doing something that cinema cannot do on its own.[6] The relationship between art and philosophy, in short, is not one of judgment and object, but rather of "resonances and interferences" across two different kinds of practice or activity, neither of which is situated "above" the other. The category of the "Baroque," which Deleuze elaborates in his book on Leibniz, for example, is a singular construct, with contemporary as well as historical uses, and with scientific as well as artistic implications—for we are still "folding, unfolding, refolding"—and the very idea of "cinema" that Deleuze develops via Bergson, in spite of that philosopher's own views about the new art, is an original one, at odds with Metzian or structuralist theory. In each case we find a complex concept "produced" by Deleuze, offering or inviting in turn nonphilosophical understandings of his own philosophy.

To do philosophy is thus to fabricate concepts in resonance and interference with the arts, past as well as present. It is never simply to apply concepts already supplied by a given theory— as Deleuze came to think had come to be the case for psychoanalysis especially when allied with linguistics. For one must always again *produce* the concepts; and a great critic is not one who comes armed with prior theory, but rather one who helps formulate new problems or suggests new concepts. There is thus a side of Deleuze's pragmatism of multiplicities that is "against theory." One can really think only where what is to be thought is not already given; and although a philosophy may thus throw off many "uses" in the arts or in criticism, it should always resist being itself cast in turn as a new theory, which, fallen from the sky, one could then just "apply." For philosophy is not theory; it is an art of plunging into this peculiar zone of "the unthought," that destabilizes clichés and ready-made ideas, in which both art and thought come alive and discover their resonances with one another.

But there is then a further complication in Deleuze's aesthetic. The concepts he draws out or produces from the arts suppose, or even help work out, his own "image of thought." His aesthetic is thus involved in a kind of "intraphilosophical" struggle; and in all his criticism, we find a peculiar procedure that consists in calling upon the arts to show philosophy the way out of the "dogmatic image of thought" under which it has labored. We have already seen this in the case of the Idiot in the Russian novel, or in the sort of "stupidity" and "hysteria" against which Flaubert directed his writing. Similarly, in his study of cinema, Deleuze declares that the highest function of cinema (as distinct from the generality of films) is to show, through the means peculiar to it, what it is to think—what the body, the brain, and "spiritual automaton" must be for it to be possible to "think the unthought"; indeed Deleuze may be said precisely to select "cinema" from out of the generality of films according to this criterion.[7] But the same procedure is found already in his study of Proust, where the term "image of thought" is first introduced. There Deleuze enlists Proust's conception of the peculiar "intelligence" of literature to rethink the Platonic image of thought, introducing a notion of "complicated time" into its conception of recollection, and a notion of "virtuality" into his doctrine of essences. The aim of such intraphilosophical procedures in Deleuze's criticism, however, is not at all "aestheticist" or "textualist." There is no attempt to abandon philosophy in favor of art or text, or to undo all the distinctions between the two—even if there arise "zones of indistinction," as Deleuze thought might be the case surrounding contemporary notions of chaos and complexity. On the contrary, the aim is to better determine the "specificity" of philosophy and what it can do. Thus there is no one "image of thought" in the arts that suffices for philosophy; and in each case, extracting the image reflects back on the particular work or its medium in an original manner.

We see this, in particular, in Deleuze's formulation of the problem of "style" in philosophy. That a philosophy always has a "style" does not erase all distinctions between it and the arts, but on the contrary, connects it to them in a new way. For in philosophy style is precisely a way of stretching language so as to attain the concepts peculiar to it.[8] As Deleuze puts it in an aside about typography or graphic design, style should never be a substitute for thinking; and indeed the best style is the one that appears to be none at all, as with the secret "volcanic line" that runs through the calm geometry of Spinoza's *Ethics*. At the same time style is a matter of the characteristic "ascesis" or "exercise" of a philosophy—as Foucault would suggest. Thus, for example, Deleuze thinks that the dialogue-form in Plato fits with the roles of "friend" and "wisdom" in the dialectical contest to ferret out the Forms from their imperfect instantiations in things or images; and that this "conceptual agon" shows relations of philosophy to Greek sports as well as theater, exposing a kind of "athleticism" of the concept and among "friends of the concept," to be found, for example, in the kind of "combative clarity" of Foucault's own style in *Discipline and Punish*. Indeed Deleuze thinks that there is no philosophy without "conceptual personae"; and yet those personae are not to be confused with fictional or artistic ones, any more than they are to be thought of as sociological types[9]—even if, as with Flaubert's Hysteric or Baudelaire's Dandy for Foucault, there may be "resonances" with new conceptual personae, or, as in the case of Duchamp or Warhol, there may arise new "zones of indistinction" in the philosophy-art relation.[10] Such conceptual personae as Descartes's Idiot or the Leibniz's Defense Attorney for God may well thus have "resonances" in the arts, as well as with social or political figures, but the problem in creating a style in philosophy is never to simply adopt such figures from other fields. Style is a matter of bending and transforming language so as to create the personae and the contest or game for those singular ideas for which there preexist neither the words nor the story, but which nevertheless press upon us with an obscure necessity.

One might thus say of Deleuze's own style—with its peculiar usage of words (including "concept" itself), its composition in series or plateaus, its disparate, seamless "smoothness" and distinctive humor—that it works to encourage "uses" while frustrating "applications," and so to serve as "interceder" inciting creation or thinking in other nonphilosophical domains. Thus it helps show in practice the "image of thought," which, we have seen, Deleuze sought in his logic and in his view of "a life." Conversely, his logic and his vitalism lead to two basic principles in his aesthetic. For in his logic, Deleuze works out a notion of "sense" prior to the establishment of codes, languages, and, in this sense, of "mediums"—all ideas that have had quite an important role in the arts and in talk about the arts. It is the logic of such sense that gives his study of signs and images in the arts a special status, irreducible to language or code. We find this not only with his analysis of signs in Proust, but also of the "images" in cinema—in each case, signs and images belong to a logic of "sense and event" rather than of truth and proposition. More generally, for Deleuze art may be said to "make sense" before it acquires significations, references, or "intentions" identified through the institutions of a public *Sinn* or a "common sense"; and a problem in his criticism is thus in each case to attain the level in which a given artwork or artform thus tries to "construct a multiplicity." Many received notions about art or the artwork, its institutions and its publics, are rethought in relation to this problematic "layer of sense," which Deleuze tries

to extract from a given work, in formulating the original conceptual problems that it poses.

But there is then a second principle. For it is just in making
such "prelinguistic, presubjective" sense that a work is able to
pose the problem of "a life" as it is deployed in the space and
time in a particular society or situation. Within each work or
each artform, there thus exists a nodal point where logic and
life—"splendid impersonality" and "vital possibility"—inter-
sect; and an aim in Deleuze's criticism is ever to discover it anew.
His criticism is thus "clinical" in a peculiar sense that philosophy shares precisely with the arts: that of what Nietzsche called
"great health" as distinct from the "good health" of comfort and
security. Indeed Deleuze is perhaps the first since Nietzsche to
find a way to practice aesthetics as a "gay science," extracting it
from Nietzsche's Alpine aphorisms and reinserting it into the
heart of urban "modernity"—into the very sense of the "modern
work" in Warhol as well as Flaubert, Burroughs as well as Kafka.
For perhaps that is the secret—to practice aesthetics as affirmative play of conceptual experimentation and novelty, and not as
tribunal and judgment.

2 In the last pages of the volumes on cinema, Deleuze
arrives at conclusions that thus capture something of
his larger conception of the artwork and, in particular, the modern artwork.[11] The thing called "cinema"
that has been the object of his study, he says, is not a language,
a narrative code or a sign-system, but rather an "intelligible material" given form through a "becoming-art"—in fact through
two different "becomings-art," each involving a distinct "regime" (but not a code or language) of images and signs: the

movement-regime and the time-regime. The idea of such a "becoming-art" is freely adapted from Alois Riegl's notion of a *Kunstwollen* or "artistic volition"; and, as with Reigl, it is opposed to any simple historical or contextualist determinism— "this study is not a history," Deleuze declares at the start of his works about "cinema." The picture of an "artistic volition" giving form to an "expressive" or "intelligible" material is developed for each of the two volumes, in a complex and often dramatic manner, and leads to the question with which the study of cinema closes—in our contemporary global tele-informational culture that tends to blur all distinctions between the artificial and the natural, what new expressive materials and becoming-art (what new "regime" of signs and images) might we yet invent?

What then does this picture involve? An intelligible "material" is not to be confused with matter or content in an already codified medium; and the "becoming-art" through which it takes shape is not to be confused with a history—it is rather the actualization in a material of new powers or forces with which to experiment. In that great industrial art, the cinema, we may thus distinguish two "regimes." Each comes from particular social and political conditions, indeed each matches with different possibilities not simply for art but also for thought and the role of the intellectual, the coming war being the larger event that marks the shift from one to the other. Yet no one could have predicted—or even fully explain in retrospect—such "becomings-art"; indeed that is just why the intervention of "artistic will" was needed. For the "will" in question was neither a sum of subjective intentions nor the expression of a collective program; it has another sense and other effects. Indeed the "I" and "we" don't come before such a "becoming-art," but on the contrary form part of its invention, its experimentation. An "artistic volition" thus starts with no given public, obeys no established "inter-subjective norms" of judgment, reduces to no sociological or institutional definition, and can be contained or directed by no avant-garde with its pope-master—such is precisely its force and its promise.

In studying the successive "regimes" of movement and time images in cinema in this way, Deleuze may then be said to work out two larger principles in his aesthetic. The first says that those who are involved in the "becoming-art" of an expressive material—who are drawn to it and transformed by it, or who invent ways to see and say new things through it—do not pre-exist it, but are rather invented in the process. If there is "will" in art, it does not belong to a known or identifiable "agency"; rather it is many different people and disciplines talking and seeing in new ways at once, interfering and resonating with one another, thanks to some as-yet unformed or uncoded material of expression. Time-images perhaps show this principle better than do movement-images. For with movement-images, which help make visible the "mechanisms of masses," one still may entertain the illusions of the sort of collective agency that might be "represented" by intellectuals—illusions that would be exploited (and ruined, claims Deleuze along with Syberberg) by Hitler. After the war, when such illusions no longer seemed credible, another kind of "becoming-art" would arise in the expressive material of cinema—one would start to show something intolerable for which there exists precisely no collective project or program, and which thus raises the question of "agency" or the "time of agency" in another manner—eventually in terms of "minorities," and the manner in which they insert "becomings" into the official histories of majorities. It is then with the time-images that come after the war that cinema, as it were, says most explicitly that "the people is missing, the people is not there," which Deleuze wants to make a more general feature of "artistic volition." It is something found earlier in other ways—in one way by Kafka in his letters, in another by Klee in the Bauhaus. Thus Deleuze will say that in all art, for all art, the people is never given and must be invented anew, and we must thus be wary, for example, of the ways in which conceptual art serves simply to "bring the concept back to the doxa of social body or of the great American metropolis."[12] As a presupposition of a "becoming-art," the people that is not yet there is not to be confused with "the public," or with transcendental intersubjective norms supposed by "the public"—on the contrary, it helps show why art (and thought) is never a matter of "communication," why for them there is always too much "communication." For what it supposes is a condition of another kind, not transcendental, but experimental. We thus discover a second feature of "artistic volition," or a second principle in the aesthetic that tries to isolate it. If art, or the "will to art," supposes a people that is missing, that is yet to come, it is because there arises in a peculiar condition—the condition in which something new may arise. One problem in Deleuze's aesthetic is then to say what this condition is and how it contrasts with the attempt to find transcendental conditions for judgment. For "novelty" in this case is not to be confused with known or visible "fashions" and the manner in which they are manipulated and promoted, but on the contrary, is something we do not or cannot yet see is happening to us, indeed something that we ourselves need to become "imperceptible" in order to see. In Deleuze's aesthetic, a "will to art" is always concerned with the emergence of something new and singular, which precedes us and requires us to "invent" ourselves as another people.

We are thus at some distance from the more traditional notions of "mediums" in art, in as much as they suppose a code or language for a preexistent subject, agent, or public. That is one reason why Deleuze found himself engaged in a struggle with certain structuralist or formalist ideas of the day, and often presented his conception of unformed expressive materials as an alternative to it. Thus against Christian Metz he argues that cinema is not in the first instance a narrative code "structured like a language," uncritically exploited by Hollywood. Rather narrative is only one consequence of the formation of the regime of movement-images; and the break from narrative is thus more than a matter of critical self-reference to a narrative code—Deleuze thought little of the whole idea of "critical self-reference," in cinema as elsewhere. The break with classical narrative is rather to be understood in terms of the emergence of another kind of cinematic "image." After the war, there is a sort of crisis in the very idea of what an "image" is, leading to the invention of the new cinematic procedures that make neo-Realism, for example, more than a return to social contents, the start of a whole new cinematic *Kunstwollen.* But it is no different for painting, often seen as the avatar of the idea of "critical self-reference" in modern work. Thus what Deleuze calls the "logic of sensation" in painting is not to be confused with a code or language of painting, of the sort of which Kandinsky or Mondrian dreamed.[13] On the contrary it works with uncoded "diagrammatic traits," which serve to create pictorial space in bodily terms that depart from the classical conception of painting as framed window.

Painting is thus unformed, presubjective "material of expression" before it is a pictorial code; and the connections between hands and eyes or faces and landscapes, which come to underlie its codes, thus do not exhaust its possibilities. Undoing such connections is moreover not a matter of critical self-reference of a medium, and the purifying or reductive notion of abstraction associated with it. In Francis Bacon's singular "ef-faced" portraits, for example, we find a "will" to express something prior to narration, figuration, or illustration, involving new kinds of spatialization and color. Painting, for Deleuze, is not the model of reductive abstraction in all the other arts that Clement Greenberg took it to be; as with Bacon's attempt to discover a nonillustrative violence of bodily space, prior to signification and subjectivity, it is more a kind of minor or foreign visual idiom in what we have been accustomed to see. That is why Deleuze is drawn to another of Klee's dicta, making it his own: "not to reproduce what we can already see, but to make visible what we cannot." For in all art there is a violence of what comes before the formation of codes and subjects, which is a condition in an expressive material of saying and seeing things in new ways.

3   What then would it mean to think of art or the work of art in its relation to such violence? Developing some ideas of Blanchot, Foucault had tried to understand the "madness" peculiar to the modern work as a kind of "absence d'oeuvre," a kind of "un-work"; in this way he rediscovers his own view of the anonymity of discourse as a condition or event, or the emergence of something new.[14] Deleuze himself often refers to this attempt, developing it in his own way—he talks about making vision or language stutter, as if speaking a foreign tongue saying ". . . and, and, and" rather than "is." But Deleuze never wanted to make a theology out of such "absence," as though it were the mark of some Law; for him it was a matter of multiplicity or construction multiplicity, not of some transcendental void or emptiness. He was never drawn to attempts to turn the voids or silences in modern work into a mystical metaphysic of the Unsayable of the Invisible. The problem he isolates in modern work, the "unwork" it would bring out in all work, is rather what he calls "possibility in the aesthetic sense—some possibility or else I'll suffocate." In a modern world of stupefying banality, routine, cliché, mechanical reproduction or automatism, the problem is to extract a singular image, a vital, multiple way of thinking and saying, not a substitute theology or "auratic object." It is a matter of creating a "plane of composition" rather than a theological plan—an organization from above or for an independent eye, a design in God's mind, an evolution from the supposed depths of nature or the powers of society. The modern work is thus "chaosmotic" in Joyce's phrase— it works through surface series and variations, as when Warhol introduces small differences into series of images, or, in another more "obsessive" way, in the nouveau roman. Even the "exhausted" bodily postures in Beckett would not be read as an ontology of the "death of God," or a substitute for a disappointed theology, but rather as a diagnosis of what body and world are when all possibilities seem "exhausted."[15] For what matters is not the "empty place" in a work, but rather this other "Spinozistic" plan that comes before the specification of forms and formation of subjects, or the problem of constructing multiplicities.

The work thus doesn't *start* with an anxious encounter with the "empty place," and it doesn't try to denude itself in preparation for a revelation or uncovering of Being. Rather it starts with probabilities and then tries to extract from them singularities brought together in another sort of compositional plan—even Mallarmé must be rethought along such lines. Thus Deleuze declares that "the painter does not paint on a virgin canvas, the writer does not write on a blank page, but the page or the canvas are already covered over with pre-existing, preestablished clichés,"[16] which must be scraped away to find a singular vital space of possibility. That space is not an untouchable void, but rather what Deleuze sometimes calls "desert," as when, in his study of Bacon, he says the aim is to "put some Sahara in the brain."[17] For the desert is populated by nomads or by a nomadic sort of chance and spatial distribution—the kind of chance that, in contrast to surrealist "probabilities," no throw of the dice can abolish. The same is true for the problem of "images" in cinema, and the way they would free themselves of ambient clichés, or, again, for the kind of "brain" Leo Steinberg already saw in Rauchenberg's composites.[18] In *Cinema 2* Deleuze declares ours in fact not a civilization of the image, but rather of the cliché, the whole problem being to extract a genuine image from it; thus we must rethink the very idea of "image" (and brain), freeing itself from any prior program, outside point of view, or fixed "gaze."[19]

Deleuze was thus never taken with the idea of some great "postmodern break"—Guattari was quite hostile to the notion. For already in the modern work the question is one not of "anxiety," absence, and Being, but of "intensity," possibility, and singularity. To the irony, skepticism, or quotationalism on which Pomo prides itself, Deleuze opposed a kind of humor of sense and nonsense, of a sort to be seen in the logic of Lewis Carroll or the pataphysics of Alfred Jarry, precursor of Heidegger—*his* idea of the "simulacrum," where one can no longer distinguish model from copy, is to be not found in "hyperrealism," but rather in Robbe-Grillet or Beckett, as earlier in the swerving atoms of Stoic physics. He thinks that in all art (or in anything worth calling "art"), we find an attempt to find release from the suffocating sense of given possibility, ready-made ideas; even in the old masters, we find a fight against immobility, catatonia— against, in a word, "depression." There is a logic to the fight— to extract possibility from probability, multiplicity from unity, singularity from generality—the logic of "a life." A basic problem for Deleuze's larger conception of aesthetics is then to introduce this sense of "intensity" into the very idea of "sensation" and our relation with it—into the very concept of "aisthesis." Instead of looking for "conditions of possibility" of sensation, we might then be able to look to sensation for the condition of other possibilities of life and thought.

4 In an appendix to his lecture on the origin of the work of art, Heidegger says that "aisthesis" is the element in which art dies, agonizing for several centuries; the craft of thinking must thus step back and rediscover the sense in which art is about truth or the disclosure of worlds.[20] Deleuze moves in another direction; his problem is not truth, but rather "possibility in the aesthetic sense"—something that, though "secret," is not hidden and then disclosed. Thus, for his part, he says that in Kant the idea of "aesthetics" divides into two—there are "forms of sensation" as conditions of possible experience, and then there is a theory of beauty (and hence art) as a kind of "reflected reality," based in a series of analogies. What happens in the modern work, regarded as "intensive," is then not only a break with such analogies, as already with the notion of the sublime in Kant. It is also a bringing together of these two sides or senses of "aesthetics" in a new way, connecting sensation with experimentation, so that "sensation is revealed in the work of art at the same time as the work appears as experimentation."[21] Or, as Deleuze puts it in a striking passage in *Difference and Repetition,* "Ariadne has hung herself. . . . [T]he work of art leaves the domain of representation to become 'experience' (or 'experiment'), transcendental empiricism or science of the sensible."[22] In the resulting "aesthetics," the figure of the experimenter thus takes over for the Kantian Judge.

What then does it mean to extract the "being of sensation" from representation and make it a matter of experimentation? One example might be the problem of the modern work, or the "madness" of the modern work, posed by Foucault—modern literature would extract a "being of language" prior to the epistemic or discursive arrangements of words and images, attaining the element of the "anonymous murmur" of discourse from which epistemes arise or into which they sink. Our relation with this "being of language" would be rather different from that of the classical period, where language was subordinated to "representation"—Foucault thought it exposes us to a peculiar madness. To extract sensation from representation is thus to discover something mad and impersonal in it, prior to the "I think" or the "we judge"—it is to extract it from the relation of subject and object still supposed in Kant's conception of "representation," and to free it from subordination to a sort of "sensus communis" Kant thought was supposed in judgment. Thus "aisthesis" attains modernity or another sense of modernity than that of a tribunal of aesthetic judgment, distinct (though nevertheless tied to) those of science and morals. We see it, for example, in those "illuminations" that make visible what cannot yet be seen or thought, or in those uncentered worlds in which such disparate or multiple "perspectives" can coexist, like many different cities in a city—a modernity, as Deleuze puts it, that prefers its *lumières* in the plural, without trying to insert them all into some overarching program called *"the Enlightenment."*

For to extract sensation from representation, making it a matter of experimentation rather than judgment, is also to free the art of seeing from its subordination to prior concept or discourse. Thus Deleuze tries to show how the modern work departs from the idea of a "schematism" linking intuition and concept. For not only is the relation between the two variable, but what links them is not a "schema" but rather conditions of another kind, from which a work can depart—as, for example, with the way in which Foucault shows that Magritte undoes precisely the classical or "representational" connection between the two. Similarly, Lyotard studied how in the modern work the relations between figure and discourse free themselves from the classical assumptions of narration and figuration.[23] Drawing in different ways on these two works, Deleuze proposes to extend Riegl's distinction between "the optic" and the "haptic."[24] He sees the two as referring to two different kinds of seeing or two different "spatializations" of vision, which concern, for example, what is taken to be near and far. "Haptic space" thus anticipates what in the "intensive space" of the modern work would depart from the figure-ground, eye-hand relations dear to Gestalt psychology—for example, the kind of "disconnected spaces" explored in modern cinema, or the problems posed by the Chinese wall in Kafka, or the strange world without "the other" in Tournier's *Friday.* In these various ways, the modern work thus divides what the Kantian schematism unites—it shows that saying and seeing do not come related as concept and intuition, form and content, or signifier and signified, as more "formalist" ideas of modernism still suppose.

To extract sensation from representation is then to take space and time and their role as "forms of intuition" that make possible the "I think" that accompanies all representation, and make them instead part of an aesthetic "experimentation." Our relation to space and time—our spatiality or temporality—changes; and the work shows the change—as it were, it exposes what in space and time is then to be "experimented with." We have already seen this for the case of time—there is a kind of temporal indetermination in the unfolding of a life, which is prior to the "I think" of representations, or the "synthesis of the manifold" on which it rests; and it is precisely this time implicated in us that cannot be put into any prior movement, linear or cyclical, which, for example, Deleuze sees cinema exploring through its time-images. But along with such "unjointed time," there goes a change in space, and our experience-experiment with space—we pass from an "extensive" to an "intensive" spatiality. We find an "ungrounded" or "ungrounding" (*effondé*) space given through an "asymmetrical synthesis of the sensible"—which departs from the "good form" of objects in milieu, as, for example, with the Kantian synthesis of the manifold.[25] For in departing from the idea of well-constituted objects-with-properties and the kinds of distance and relation they suppose, one departs from the idea of extension (of a space divisible *partes ex partes*). Deleuze then discovers a kind of amorphous or unformed space, shown through "anexact" diagrams of pregeometric figures, in which Husserl saw the origins of geometry.[26] Deleuze thinks Husserl should have extended his phenomenology to such spaces, rather than making them part of the genesis of good geometric figures.

For what the modern work shows is that we have very different bodily or kinesthetic relations with "intensive" than we do with "extensive" spatiality. We *move* in space in ways that cannot be mapped by any "extension"; we "fill it out" according to informal diagrams that do not completely organize it, such that the space and our movements in and through it become inseparable from one another—as, for example, Deleuze thinks Deligny explored in mapping the movements of autistic children, or Paul Klee suggested in his *Pedagogical Sketchbooks*—and we must ask what our body and our brains or minds must be if we are capable of such an "intensive" or "experimental" spatiality. "Intensive space" takes us beyond the forms of the "lived body" described by phenomenology.

In some ways, phenomenology accompanies the arts in the effort to rescue "sensation" from enclosure in representation, or its subordination to the subject of representation; Henri Maldiney, for example, shows how the arts depart from the role Hegel assigned sensation at the start of his phenomenology of the *Gestalten* of Spirit.[27] But Deleuze thinks there remains a Kantian element in phenomenology—it, as it were, reinserts transcendence into the "life-world," and so retains something of the poisoned gift of transcendental philosophy; it still wants conditions of judgment rather than of experimentation. It is precisely this element of transcendence that it then calls upon the arts to show us. Phenomenology still *needs* the arts to "disclose the world," whose conditions it then describes, a kind of Urdoxa in which the "flesh" of the world and the body would coincide, for example. Thus Merleau-Ponty needs Cézanne to show "things themselves," whereas Francis Bacon takes the "logic of sensation" further—no longer to the quasi-spiritual world of "the flesh," but rather to the violence of "the meat."

"Tender is the flesh," says Deleuze of phenomenology.[28] For sensation becomes fully a matter of experimentation only when it is no longer enclosed in the transcendental conception of the world that phenomenology still tries to discern—when the possibilities of "a life" are freed from the phenomenological "life-world," and the ways it serves to condition perception.

We see this, in particular, with the role of "affect" as a kind of sensation, particularly important in music, and so also in dance. We have seen that what Deleuze calls the immanence of a life is not to be confused with the mysticism of an advent of Being we must await with patience and piety. His problem of "intensity" is thus not that of the anxiety as a preliminary to our access to Being, just as piously awaiting its revelation or disclosure is not his idea of our dignity. The problem in Deleuze's experimentalist aesthetic is the sense of "suffocation" against which the search for "possibility in the aesthetic sense" is always directed; and the basic affect through which this sense is given is depression or what Spinoza called "the sad passions"—for, as Jacques Lacan remarks, Spinoza turns depression into a kind of ethical failing.[29] Affect in Spinoza becomes the sensation of what favors or prevents, augments or diminishes, the powers of life of which we are capable each with one another; and it is in something of this same "ethical" sense that Deleuze proposes to extract clinical categories (like "hysteria" or "perversion" or "schizophrenia") from their legal and psychiatric contexts and make them a matter of experimentation in modes of life in art and philosophy, or as categories of a philosophico-aesthetic "clinic." Before our Prozac world, Freud tried to understand "melancholy" (and its relations with the arts) in terms of the work of mourning concerning loss or absence. But Deleuze thinks there is a "unmourning" that requires more work, but promises more joy. Considered in philosophico-aesthetic terms, melancholy might then be said to be the sensation of an unhappy idealization, and the real antidote to it is to be found not in rememorization and identification, but in active forgetting and affirmative experimentation with what is yet to come.

5   In the cinema volumes, Deleuze develops this idea of sensation as experiment and clinic of vital possibilities in another way—in relation to the nervous system, or as a kind of "neuroaesthetic." The central ideas of "image" and "sign" in his study of cinema are elaborated not through the marriage of psychoanalysis and linguistics, but rather through the nerve-science contemporary with the emergence of cinema, from which psychoanalysis arose. Thus in Bergson he finds an original "philosophy of the brain" opposed to the idea of reflex in our ideas of memory and action; and the shift from movement-images to time-images in cinema may then be seen as a shift from one kind or one conception of the brain to another—from a kinesthetic or movement brain to the brain as a kind of "uncertain system" that works through "irrational breaks."[30] Thus time emerges as such (as "unjointed") just when cinema departs from a world of action and reaction, found, for example, in the kind of fast "reflex-brain" of American film, and, as it were, concerns itself with all that happens in between stimulus and response. But the relation between nervous systems, artistic sensations, and philosophical "psychologies" goes beyond such "resonances" with cinema. The idea of "sensation" in modern painting, for example, may be understood in this context; and an important philosophical work remains the *Principles of Psychology* of William James (who was no stranger to the

problem of depressive affect and the mobility of things in the making). In James as with Bergson, philosophy seemed to go with writing and art (the "stream of consciousness," for example); and a basic focus of such "neuroaesthetics" was on nervous disorders and conditions in the modern city. The cinema volumes then offered Deleuze a way of pursuing the clinic of "sensation," whose logic in painting he had posed in his study of Francis Bacon.

When in *What Is Philosophy?* Deleuze says that "art is sensation and nothing else," he is trying to capture an idea that runs through his work; and the term "sensation" is to be understood in terms of the resulting idiom. In this idiom, "sensation" is not determined by representation, and is expressed through images and signs of another kind, which make of it a "transcendental empiricism" or aesthetic experimentation with what is singular or new. Sensations are thus not to be confused with subjective states or with "sensibilia" or "sensationalism." On the contrary, Deleuze is impressed when, against the Impressionists, Cézanne says that the sensations are in things themselves, not in us; and he sees the violence of Bacon's "sensations" as directed precisely against the clichés of a photographic sensationalism. Affects and percepts are the two basic types of sensation, of which the artwork may be said to be a composite. But the first, with which music and dance are especially concerned, are not to be confused with personal feelings, just as the second, to be found literature as well as the visual arts, are not to be confused with objects given to a perceiving subject. Rather, as in what Freud called "unconscious emotions" such as feelings of guilt, affects go beyond the subjects that pass through them, and they are impersonal, even inhuman; and percepts are not ways of presenting nature to an eye, but are rather like landscapes, urban as well as natural, in which one must lose oneself so as to see with new eyes, as, for example, with Mrs. Dalloway. We thus have peculiar relations with the sensations we call "art." Materials become expressive (or unfold a "will-to-art" or "becoming-art") just when they realize sensations of this sort; and, conversely, the aim of art is, through expressive materials, to extract sensations from habitual sensibilia—from habits of perception, memory, recognition, agreement—and cause us to see and feel in new or unforeseen ways. The composite of sensations that is the work of art (or the work in art) is then not to be confused with its material support (as with minimalist ideas of the "medium"), nor with techniques (as in the informational idea of a medium). It is a peculiar thing, which precedes and may survive the physical supports and technological means without which it would nevertheless not exist.

Art not only extracts such "sensations." It also puts them in a kind of construction; and every work has an architecture, even if askew or non-Euclidean. Thus art is less the incarnation of a lifeworld than a strange construct we inhabit only through transmutation or self-experimentation, or from which we emerge refreshed as if endowed with a new optic or nervous system. A painting is such a construct rather than an incarnation—indeed that is just why it can depart from the eye-hand-nature or facelandscape relations associated with phenomenological incarnation. But with cinema regarded as a kind of "spiritual automaton" or "psycho-mechanics," the question of sensation is posed in another way, starting, for example, with Bergon's distinction between habitual and attentive recognition.[31] But in cinema we see that this problem of "attention" soon leads us away from what can be contained in kinesthetic milieus, and poses the question of another kind of seeing or *voyance*. A new kind of brain is required, capable of dealing with zones of indistinction between stimulus and response and the strange unjointed sense of continuity and time that comes from them. That is what cinema explores from many angles—with the problem of colors in Antonioni, or of trauma in Resnais, for example. More generally, it is through such a neuroaesthetic brain that cinema diagnoses new spaces and times in the postwar European city, as earlier with the metropolitan "modernity" of which Baudelaire saw painting as the search. The general problem of "possibility in the aesthetic sense," in other words, assumes a neurological cast with a clinical or diagnostic side; and it is in this regard that Deleuze turns back to Pierre Janet to understand mechanical "automatisms," and then raises the question of the informational ones, which Godard and Syberberg would start to diagnose in their cinematic critiques of "information-society." The neuroaesthetic problem of sensation may then be put in this way: either to create new connections, new linkages, or vital "transmitters" in the brain, or else to fall back into a kind of "deficiency of the cerebellum," a debility of the sort one experiences in bad cinema, and a fortiori in the "world-as-bad-cinema" with which Serge Daney thought television had come to confront us.[32]

Neuroaesthetics becomes possible, in other words, just when sensation is freed from representation and even from phenomenological conditions to become experimental and diagnostic. And yet in neurosciences we find the tendency to reintroduce into the brain precisely the "cognitivist" schemes for recognizing objects, or else phenomenological ones for "embodying" life-worlds, from which, in Deleuze's view, the "sensations" in modern artworks helped to free us—with their unformalized "optical unconscious," for example. For in attaining the "inten-

sive space" and an "unjointed time" of a life the modern work
realized in expressive materials precisely that in sensation for
which there preexist no cognitive skills and no phenomenological *Gestalten;* and, conversely, as sensation was thus opened to
experimentation, the brain became a matter for philosophy and
art as well as for science. It acquired a "diagnostic" role, which
neuroscientists miss when they reintroduce into their understanding of art and our relation to it the old schemes of representation, allegory, symbolism, iconography. The problem of
drugs and the brain in artistic creation, for example, must be understood in relation to "sensations" or "intensities," more as the
mark of a failure to make a "construct" out of them than as a
privileged mode of access to them. Thus, as Deleuze puts it, neuroscience doesn't in fact tell us how will we think or feel, but
only what our brains must be for it to be possible for us to think
and feel in other new ways.[33]

The problem concerning information-society or the "brain-
city" with which Deleuze leaves us in the last pages of the cinema volumes is of this neuroaesthetic sort. In many ways the
problems explored by moderns were "mechanical" kinds of automatism, and release from the kind of stultifying "segmented"
spaces that went with them. But with our societies of informa-
tion-type machines, the problem changes. It becomes a matter
of a "control" rather than of such segmentalizing "discipline,"
more insidious because more flexible, more random, more
spread-out and "smooth."[34] One indication is the problem of
"achievement" skills, and the mad competition to survive by ac-
quiring them. Our problem is no longer so much one of the
"behaviorism" that arose together with the new sciences of
discipline as of cognition or "intelligence" that has become the
object of a sort of cognitive Darwinism of cerebral skills,

working independently of cultures or locales. What new *Kunst-wollen,* Deleuze seems to be asking, might we yet invent today to diagnose the maladies in this new information-achievement-cognitivism and give us the sensations—and the brains—to again breathe the fresh air of "possibility in the aesthetic sense"?

6   Artworks are composed of sensations, prelinguistic and presubjective, brought together in an expressive material through a construct with an anorganized plan, with which we have peculiar relations. They are not there to save us or perfect us (or to damn or corrupt us), but rather to complicate things, to create more complex nervous systems no longer subservient to the debilitating effects of clichés, to show and release the possibilities of a life. Deleuze thinks this is true for apparently theological works like "The Burial of Count Orgaz," which follow the principle that "God exists, therefore everything is permitted";[35] and Francis Bacon's own Catholicism may be read in terms of his world of "meat-sensations" (rather than the other way around), much as the cries of the damned in Leibniz's Baroque theology may be seen from the perspective of a coexistence of different possible worlds, that departs from harmony or perfection and so from a God who selects the best, from which, as it were, they are kept in "damning" themselves. For in the first instance our relation with the sensations we call art is not defined by some higher realm or "transcendence"; and what they afford us is neither salvation nor *eudaimonia,* but rather what Nietzsche called a "higher health." The opposite of the kind of "suffocation" they combat, in other words, is not contentment or "happiness," but rather the vitality and mobility that is the only true antidote to melancholy as

affect of an unattainable idealization or "hope"—thus they rewire the nervous system, revitalize the brain, releasing us, in mind as in body, from the heaviness of grounded identities and habitual forms. That, at any rate, may be said to be the principle in Deleuze's "aesthetic clinic" and of its "materialism." It is what distinguishes it from the idealizing piety of art as Kantian "disinterest" (even when recast as Heideggerian *Gelassenheit*), or as Freudian "sublimation" (even when reformulated as the empty place of *das Ding*), as well as from the strange, sensual-spiritualist side of French phenomenology, which Deleuze sees as growing up around the Christian theme of "the flesh."[36] For in such views we find, in effect, aesthetic versions of transcendence—with Nietzsche one might say of "ascetic ideals" and the "sad passions" that accompany them. Against such aesthetic pieties, we must push sensation beyond transcendence where it becomes a matter of belief not in another world, but in "other possibilities" in this one.

The problem of such "belief-in-the-world" in the arts may be said to be raised by William James in his attempt to find a "will to believe" as a philosophical antidote to depression as quasi-religious affect, and, more generally, his attempt to invent a "pragmatism" in which questions of experimentation and chance would replace those of salvation and judgment.[37] But Deleuze thinks that the problem is pursued in other ways—for example, by Godard's cinematic attempt to replace the question of belief in God or in the Revolution with an exploration of the "worlds" or "modes of existence" supposed by such beliefs in transcendence.[38] In this Godard would go further than Pascal in his wager. For if Pascal substitutes for the question of belief the question of the modes of existence of the believer and non-believer, Godard belongs to those who reinsert the wager into a world of chance and indetermination, where one can no longer calculate the probabilities—where, as Deleuze puts in those pages of *Difference and Repetition* devoted to the question of belief, the world is ever still "making itself" such that God's calculations (as well as ours) never come out quite right.[39] To attain this belief or trust in the world, prior to divine calculation, and so to any judgment or judgment-day, is then what Deleuze calls an "empiricist conversion."[40] It is precisely such a belief or trust that cinema managed to give us after the "trauma" of the war, from which artists and thinkers had to return, as if from the dead; and is what, in relation to the new questions of the "information-society" and its cult of "communication," Deleuze came to think we need most.[41]

In *Difference and Repetition,* Deleuze tries to work out what such belief supposes—a sense of a what is "to come," or the "synthesis of time" concerned not with the regularities of the present or the indeterminacy of the past, but rather with a "belief of the future, in the future."[42] He says that it is in fact "religious thinkers" like Pascal, Kierkegaard, and Péguy who have spoken best of this "time to come," and the way it differs from the eternal or the transient. But we must "empirically convert" this still religious sense of time, making it a matter of sensation and experimentation, and so of "aisthesis" and aesthetics, in this world that is not yet "our" world. For when there is no such belief, no such "aisthesis," we find nihilism, formulated by Nietzsche, introduced into cinema by Orson Welles or into literature by Herman Melville[43]—it is only despair that we say "the people is missing, the people is not there"; then there arises a sense that all identities are "counterfeit," and a tendency to fall back on some "myth of a past people" as the source of original identity.

In some sense that is already Deleuze's diagnosis of Plato's poisoned gift of transcendence—that when doxa is problematized, making thought necessary, there is a tendency to enclose it within some rediscovered transcendence, some prior, purer "plan of organization"—just the mysticism that counters such a "theological" plan with a primal Void or Absence fits with what Nietzsche said of nihilism, that we prefer to believe in nothing than not to believe at all. In the problematizing situation from which philosophy derives, we need rather to change the nature of belief itself, freeing it from such Urdoxa; we need to think of it not in terms of "higher knowledge," but in terms of the kind of "trust in the world" offered us by those strange sensations-constructs we call art, and the kind of health or vitality with which they are concerned.

A lament starts to emerge in Deleuze's writings, as his own phystic condition overtook him. Already in his study of cinema, he sensed that the kind of "belief in the world" that, following the Second World War, cinema had found a way to give us was no longer well adapted to our situation, that it was in turn losing its "credibility" or "credit." We find a retreat of thought back into transcendence, reformulated as "communication" or "information," so that, confronted with the new "stupidity" and "automatism" of our information-societies, the violence of those excluded from them, as well as the new "becomings" they might yet unleash, we are presented with philosophies of consensus, at once naive and self-assured. Thus we were entering an impoverished time for the creation of philosophy, as if one had to cross the desert to be able to carry it on anew; and what we require is a new Ariadne, adapted to societies of control, working in and with the electronic brain-city, capable of saying "yes" to what is strange and singular in our existence, inciting an art and will to art, a taste for fresh sensations and constructions of sensation. For what we lack is not communication (we have too much of that), but rather this belief in what we may yet become, and in the peculiar time and logic of its effectuation in ourselves and in our relations with one another. That may make fools laugh, said Deleuze—the whole problem is to believe in a world that includes them.

Chapter 1

1. MP, p. 634.

2. MP, p. 13.

3. "What is a *dispositif?*" in *Michel Foucault, Philosopher,* ed. Timothy Armstrong (Routledge, 1992), p. 165.

4. K, p. 146.

5. See Claude Imbert, *Pour une histoire de la logique* (PUF, 1999) for a view of another history of logic that would include this other sort of sense, drawing on her earlier discussion of Frege and Merleau-Ponty in *Phénoménologies et langues formulaires* (PUF, 1992). Both Wittgenstein's and Merleau-Ponty's last writings were about color—about the multifaceted "grammar" of our talk of it and about the non-Cartesian, nonperspectival "sense" it would acquire with Cézanne. Both might thus be read together usefully with the Deleuze's view of logic of color not as property of thing, but as original spatializing "infinitive" in *Logic of Sense,* where, as Claude Imbert puts it, the question becomes what color does in a perceptual world that, according to Lewis Carroll, has lost its "Euclidean skin" (unpublished ms.). Deleuze pursues this question of the logic of color in his study of Bacon, as well as, for example, in his account of Antonioni as a "colorist" in cinema.

6. SPP, p. 122.

7. Michel Foucault, "Theatrum Philosophicum" in *Dits et Ecrits* (Gallimard, 1994), pp. 94ff; on thinking as "perilous act," see *The Order of Things* (Random House, 1970), p. 328.

8. C2, p. 33. The same idea is elaborated by Deleuze in his treatment of the problem of photography in Francis Bacon, who kept lots of photo images in his studio (LS, p. 13; and 65ff, on

the question of the canvas is always covered-over with clichés). Perhaps more generally the habit of collecting photographs and other images by painters might be read in terms of a Flaubertian "stupidity" of the archive and the "violence" of the procedures to escape from it—Deleuze's gloss on Leo Steinberg's "other criterion" of nonverticality as the distinctive feature of a possible *Kunstwollen* in the new regime of electronic images (see C2, p. 349, note 11) might be read in this way.

9. See C2, p. 354, note 21 to Raymond Ruyer's *La cybernétique et l'origine de l'information*, where the problem is related to procedures of "framing" and "unframing" Deleuze studies in cinema. The question of unframing (décadrage) seems to go beyond feedback mechanisms or recursive functions—cf. QP, pp. 177ff.

10. PP, p. 246.

11. Isaac Joseph in his "Gabriel Tarde: le monde comme féerie" develops Deleuze's idea of Tarde as inventor of microsociology—in opposition to Durkheim's holism and historicism, Tarde discovers another kind of space and time of belief and desire (reprinted and expanded in *Oeuvres de Gabriel Tarde*, vol. 4, pp. 9ff, ed. Eric Alliez, Empecheurs de penser en rond, 1999, which contains several other Deleuze-inspired essays). As Joseph remarks, John Dewey's student, Robert Park, who first helped introduced Tarde together with Simmel in America, found in his notion of imitation something akin to the theme of sympathy in Hume.

12. The problem of such a space and time is already posed in 1903 by Georg Simmel, when he declares that the *Geist* of the metropolis "is to found in that fact that particularity and incomparability which every person possesses in some way is actually expressed and given life." *Individuality and Social Form* (Chicago, 1971), p. 335. The metropolis thus poses a question

central to Simmel's thought rather different from that of individuality and equality involved in classical social contract theory. One might thus see in it an anticipation of the problem of "singular community" later elaborated by Jean-Luc Nancy, which, though also not based in classical individualism, doesn't yet lead to fusion or "organic community." For Nancy proposes to see this principle at work even in an American sprawl-city like Los Angeles, declaring that the question of the city is the non-Heideggerian ethos of a "place where there takes place what has no place." *La ville au loin* (Mille et une nuits, 1999), p. 45. But Simmel is perhaps closer to Deleuze when, under the influence of Bergson, he formulates the question of such "transindividuality" instead through the principle that "transcendence is immanent in life" (p. 362).

13. PP, p. 234.

Chapter 2

1. ES, pp. 120ff. Deleuze's own empiricism breaks with the tabula rasa, and tries to "complicate" the conception of innate ideas—indeed Deleuze finds a link between empiricism and the neo-Platonic idea of a *complicatio* prior to everything that participates in Forms, shown, for example, in Whitehead (cf. QP, p. 101: ". . . the very special Greekness of English philosophy, its empirical Neo-Platonism"). Thus in Deleuze's empiricism, we don't write on a blank tablet; instead we are always "starting in the middle" of a kind of loose unfinished patchwork, itself capable of changing shape through accretion of new elements, new connections. Cf. D, pp. 54ff. The "problem of subjectivity" is then posed in a new way: it becomes a question of an artifice and an invention for which there preexists no form, no original "nature" (ES, pp. 90–92: "how, in the given, can there be

constituted a subject such that it goes beyond the given?").
More precisely, it becomes a problem of the relation of such
artifice and invention to belief.

2. William James, *A Pluralist Universe* (Nebraska, 1996),
p. 263. This lecture on Henri Bergson was directed at once against
the "totalities" of the British Hegelians and the logical "atoms"
that were then being opposed to them. Radical empiricism involves another "pluralist" logic, based neither in totalities nor
atoms—that of what Bergson called "qualitative multiplicities."

3. "Hume," in PI.

4. "Immanence: a life" in PI. Cf. Example III in QP, where
Deleuze declares (p. 49): "It is when immanence is no longer immanent to anything other than itself that we can speak of a plane
of immanence. Such a plane is perhaps a radical empiricism. . . ."

5. "Structuralism and Post-Structuralism," in *Michel Foucault, Essential Works, Vol. 2* (The New Press, 1998), p. 438.
Against Husserl, Deleuze was nevertheless drawn to Sartre's
"decisive" idea of the "transcendence of the ego." See LS, p. 120.

6. MP, pp. 95ff. Deleuze never saw himself as poststruc-
turalist. In his answer to the question "what is structuralism?"
in 1967 (*La philosophie* tome 4, ed. François Châtelet, Hachette,
1972), he discerns rather a kind of tension within structuralism;
thus the Humean idea that relations are external to their terms
would allow for his own logic of free differences and repeatable
singularities.

7. For this view of pragmatism as a philosophy of the "making" of ourselves and our world in contrast to philanthropy, see
CC, pp. 110ff.

8. "What is a dispostif?" in *Michel Foucault, Philosopher*
(Routledge, 1992). Deleuze opposes such "pluralism" to Habermas's three-way division of reason into "quasi-transcendental

interests," declaring that Foucault had become the victim of misunderstanding for which he was not responsible. Deleuze's "pluralism" might thus be related to John Dupré's thesis that the disunity of sciences supposes a disorder of things (*The Disorder of Things,* Harvard, 1993)—Dupré's "disorder" would be something like "chaos" in the philosophical rather than scientific sense, which Deleuze elaborates in QP. The French philosopher of science Raymond Ruyer (frequently cited by Deleuze) might then be read as offering one picture of a "disordered universe" and its relation to "frames of information" introduced by various styles of reasoning.

9. D, pp. vi–vii. Deleuze declares that "empiricism is fundamentally linked to a logic—a logic of multiplicities (of which relations are only one aspect)." One might count that view as a principle of his own empiricism; Whitehead's principles that "the abstract doesn't explain, but must itself be explained; and the aim is not to rediscover the eternal or the universal, but to find the conditions under which something new is produced (creativeness)," then, expressed the changed role of the idea of "critique" in Deleuze's experimentalism. For example, Deleuze sees a kind of "empiricism" or "experimentalism" in Foucault's critical attempt to put "abstractions" that we take for granted in our practices, such as the sick anatomy or the abnormal personality, back into the multiplicities from which they derive, thus at once complicating and "eventalizing" our history—Deleuze would say, opening it to a kind of experimentation. Cf. Foucault's own remarks on "eventalizing history" (*Dits et écrits* IV, pp. 23ff).

10. Rorty abandoned his youthful enthusiasm for Whitehead, when he took the "linguistic turn," and set out to replace all "natural philosophy" with "cultural history." Along just such

lines he tried later to deliver Dewey from the naturalistic assumptions in his concept of experience. But Rorty's "cultural history" is often thin and second-hand; and with it, he is led to a point where he is proud to no longer be able to distinguish science from literature—an odd outcome for empiricism. Dewey objected to the "spectator theory of knowledge," but what would he have thought of the "conversation theory" to which Rorty is led? For a view of "empiricism" in James and in pragmatism, closer to Deleuze's own views and in explicit contrast to Rorty, see David Lapoujade, *William James: Empirisme et pragmatisme* (PUF, 1997).

11. In "Hume" in PI, Deleuze finds the *Dialogues on Natural Religion* to be "perhaps the only case of a real dialogue in philosophy," since "there are not two characters, but three; and they don't have univocal roles, but form alliances, break them, then reconcile. . . ." Thus, to Rorty's idea of conversation, he prefers Simmel's idea of a kind of sociability prior to any particular content or agreement (QP, p. 84); and he says of Socrates that he was in fact always making "discussion" impossible, introducing things that were "undiscussable" in ordinary conversation, just because they were concerned with philosophical problems (QP, pp. 32–33).

12. CC, p. 110: "not a puzzle whose pieces in fitting together would reconstitute a whole, but more like a wall of free non-cemented stones, in which each element counts on its own, yet in relation to the others. . . ."

13. PP, p. 122. It is such "empiricist naiveté" that Deleuze imagines Foucault might have had in mind when he declared that "the century will be Deleuzian."

14. QP, p. 14. Deleuze's dismissal of the first Hegelian then Heideggerian theme of the end of philosophy is constant. In

D12, for example, he says the real Heidegger-question in post-war French philosophy is not so much Heidegger's evident Nazism; it is rather his injection of the melancholy themes like "the end of metaphysics" into the brains of a generation. Deleuze's "empiricism" formed part of his way out of this Heideggerian impasse. Thus, for example, he turns to Victor Goldschmidt for a view of Stoicism quite unlike Heidegger's, closer to his own empiricism (cf. LS, pp. 167ff).

15. PP, p. 122.

16. For a detailed contrast between Spinoza and Hobbes concerning the difference between private thinker and public professor, see Etienne Balibar, "L'institution de la vérité: Hobbes et Spinoza" in *Lieux et noms de la vérité* (Paris, Aube, 1994), pp. 21–54.

17. PP, p. 129; cf. pp. 142ff.

18. In "Nietzsche" in PI, Deleuze describes the passage from camel to lion to child, figure of innocence.

19. DR, pp. 118ff; and on Kierkegaard and Péguy, pp. 126ff.

20. "Societies of control" in PP, pp. 240ff.

21. On erehwon as "secret of empiricism," see DR, pp. 3–4. On the idea of convention in relation to rules, and as a matter of institution rather than contract, see ES, pp. 55ff and QP, p. 101. I suggest that, in effect, Deleuze wants to substitute for the old utopia-allegory relation in critical thought a diagnostic-experimental one, involving a different sort of mapping—see my "A New Pragmatism?" in *Anyhow* (MIT Press, 1998).

Chapter 3

1. "Hume" in PI.

2. QP, pp. 50–51.

3. CC, pp. 170–171.

4. DR, pp. 169ff, with a question at the end of pp. 216–218.

5. QP, Example IV, pp. 60–61.

6. Quoted in Ray Monk, *Ludwig Wittgenstein: The Duty of Genius* (Penquin, 1990). For the myriad "investigations" into which the conceptual persona in Wittgenstein's second philosophy is plunged, one might take the Shakespearean motto Wittgenstein adopted for his *Remarks on Psychology*—"I show you the differences." Thus one might speak of an "Idiot of the differences" as a persona expressing an image of thought which reorients philosophy around new problems (what it is to follow a rule), the creation of new concepts ("grammar," "form of life"), and new rivals (logicism, behaviorism); and it is precisely this persona who is then shown through an idiosyncratic style of life, or through peculiar "existential features" now recounted in many anecdotes. The endless "remarks" and "investigations" with which Wittgenstein mercilessly multiplies language so as to "show the differences," in other words, would comprise not only an original conceptual *paidea* carried on in a foreign land and tongue; it would also be a kind of "therapy," which would come to seem quite literally vital to him ("my philosophy divides in two—the part that is written and the part that is not"). A great strength of Monk's fine biography is to see the philosopher's life in terms of this invention of an original "conceptual persona" rather than the other way around.

7. QP, pp. 90–91.

8. "Theatrum Philosophicum," in *Michel Foucault Essential Works*, vol. 2 (The New Press, 1998), pp. 343ff.

9. On America and Russia, see "Bartleby" (CC, pp. 113–224), and QP, pp. 94–95, where American pragmatism and Russian socialism are presented as two ultimately disap-

pointed and disappointing attempts to revive the "Greek dream" and reconstitute a "democratic dignity." In modern capitalism, the idea of a "society of brothers" would take the place of the Greek image of a "society of friends." Along such lines, Deleuze sees Soviet-style socialism and pragmatism as each providing a different sort of "reterritorialization" for those without qualities in the modern city, such as the unlanded "proletariat" with its dreams of revolution—as it were, two places for Ulysses to return (emigrés of the world or workers of the world unite!). Our problem today is that neither form of "brotherhood" or "solidarity" is quite credible any longer; after war and fascism, and in relation to the new displacements of global capitalism, we thus need to invent new figures of "friend" (and so of "foe"). On the attempts, in the encounter with "non-Western cultures," to pose philosophical questions "freed from Hegelian and Heideggerian stereotypes," Deleuze mentions not only Levinas for Jewish thought, but also a series of authors writing on Islamic, Hindu, Chinese, and Japanese traditions. QP, p. 88, note 5.

10. QP, pp. 83–48.

11. QP, pp. 95–96. But "utopia is not a good concept," and we must push the connection of thought to the present to the point of an experimentation for which history offers only the "negative conditions" (p. 106).

12. On the link between university and state in post-Kantian philosophy, see MP, pp. 465ff.

13. QP, p. 70.

14. QP, p. 54.

15. PP, p. 206.

16. "Theatrum Philosophicum," pp. 361–362.

17. PP, p. 122.

Chapter 4

1. LS, p. 145.

2. LS, p. 135; cf. p. 32. "The logic of sense is completely inspired by empiricism," since beyond the given, it finds not essences or conditions but rather problems that express other possibilities of thought.

3. PP, p. 201.

4. CC, pp. 119ff. Jarry's tempo-mobiles not only supply a humorous angle on Heidegger's pronouncements on metaphysical essence of technology; they also fit with a series of paradoxical surreal or dada machines (Man Ray, Duchamp, Tanquely) in Deleuze's writings. See "Bilan-Programme" in AO, pp. 463–487, esp. pp. 476ff, where the principle of "uncoupling from the procedure of recurrence" allows for chance in the machine, and in particular, the city-machine relation; by contrast, when a technology is assumed to act by itself, it tends to take on a fascist color (p. 480). The relation of such machines to the Outside, supposing a certain idea of delay or time, offers a rather different picture than the many modules in the Fodorian mind, or more generally with "connectivism."

5. QP, p. 197. In neuroscience Deleuze was drawn to Steven Rose, who, placing the computer within a larger history of brain-machine analogies, proposes instead to conceive of it as a kind of probabilistic brain-system.

6. LS, p. 174. The "dignity" that consists in being equal to (*digne de*) the event in what happens to us may be said to be the basic ethical problem in philosophy, as Deleuze conceives of it. See QP, p. 151.

7. SPP. On the new relation of thought and life see chapter 1; on the role of common notions in "practical philosophy," see chapter 5.

8. CC, p. 171.

9. "To reverse Platonism," appendix I, LS, pp. 292ff.

10. D, pp. vii–viii.

11. QP, pp. 128ff. The term "logic" is sometimes used in a negative way to refer to the image of thought that would underlie the sentential logic of Frege and Russell—for example, when Deleuze talks in an added appendix of an "anti-logical machine" in Proust.

12. On the two kinds of continuity, see C2, pp. 235ff; in note 46, p. 236, Deleuze refers to Albert Spaier's distinction between rational and irrational numbers as breaks in a continuum.

13. DR, pp. 52–59.

14. On the relation of "vagueness" in Peirce to a sort of "untamed" (nomadic) chance, see Ian Hacking, *The Taming of Chance* (Cambridge, 1990), chapters 17 and 23. Similarly, Deleuze makes much of a letter of Leibniz to Arnauld in which he distinguishes between the creation of Adam-the-sinner and of the world in which Adam sins (LS, p. 134), thus opening the question of the sense of a "vague Adam" (LS, pp. 139ff). This leads Deleuze to an original view of the concept of "compossibility" in Leibniz, reducible neither to logical consistency nor causal coherence (LS, pp. 200ff).

15. PP, pp. 64–66.

16. PP, p. 194.

17. On the notion and logic of series, see LS, pp. 50ff; on the contrast with sets, see PP, pp. 79–80.

18. Saul Kripke, *Wittgenstein on Rules and Private Language* (Harvard, 1982). Goodman's "grue" paradox was meant to establish the existence of "entrenched predicates" in all inductive or predictive inference. Deleuze's notion that our "singularities" are "preindividual" might then be put by saying that they

come before the more or less entrenched "qualities" or predicates that make us predictable, introducing another kind of chance and risk into our lives, or another noninductive "synthesis of time." The public-private distinction must be rethought accordingly, as Deleuze suggests in his discussion of Whitehead (PLI, pp. 106ff). As to what this supposes concerning the idea of rules, see ES, pp. 59ff.

19. Deleuze thinks Hume introduces a "modern skepticism" that is no longer based in sensible appearances and the problem of error of the senses; the starting point is rather relations and the problem is not of error but "illusion"—of how to distinguish illegitimate from legitimate belief. See "Hume" in PI.

20. Ludwig Wittgenstein, *Culture and Value* (ed. G. H. von Wright, trans. Peter Winch, Chicago, 1980). On Deleuze's distinction between "rational" and "irrational" continuities, see C2, p. 235; and on the replacement of a crystalline for a "Euclidean" image of time, see CC, pp. 167ff.

21. B, p. 101. This idea of "invention" is connected to themes of intuition and problem in Bergson.

22. CC, p. 110.

23. MP, p. 594. The other "smooth" way of "weaving a discourse" might be said to be a feature of Deleuze's own style.

24. On perplication, see DR, 324ff and 359ff. I discuss the logic of the "pli-" words in my *Constructions* (MIT, 1998).

25. CC, pp. 180ff.

26. DR, pp. 269ff.

27. Foucault's "regularities" of discourse (like those of Wittgensteinian "grammar") are thus unlike those studied by linguistics, logicians, or speech act theorists—they suppose, says Foucault, that before it is linguistic or logical, discourse is always an event.

28. The idea of "libidinal virtuality" in Freud is developed in DR, pp. 131ff. Even in this book, one might say that Deleuze thinks that the "virtual order" we form with one another as singular libidinal beings is prior to any "symbolic order" given by our identifications and our "imaginary" relations to it. It has another "differential" logic, and another relation to the real—for example, that of relations of trait, zone, and function rather than image, subject, and imitation that Deleuze sees in the American novel (CC, pp. 100ff).

29. MP, 454ff. I discuss problem of "origins of geometry" in my *Constructions* (op. cit.).

30. Michel Foucault, *Dis et Ecrits,* p. x.

31. See MP, pp. 502ff, for the example of metallurgy, and pp. 495ff for the principle that the "sense" of an instrument is only to be found in the larger (social) "arrangement" in which it figures. The principle applies, in particular, to the electronic-informational type of machine, as Deleuze says in PP, pp. 237 and 244ff. One might then be able to distinguish "phyla" in the evolution of our various "arrangements" with types of instruments.

32. F, pp. 139–141.

33. In QP, pp. 196ff, Deleuze sketches a notion of the brain that would not only depart from a classical "logic of recognition" of objects, but also from the Gestalt and phenomenological views that were opposed to it. One should rather envisage a "nonobjectivizable" brain, the conditions for which might then be illuminated through microbiology.

34. See "Bilan-programme" in AO, pp. 463ff; on Alfred Jarry and Heidegger, see also CC, pp. 121ff.

35. See D, pp. 59ff.

36. LS, pp. 203ff. Deleuze says that Leibniz's monadic perspectivism supposes a convergence, like different points of view

on the same city. In Nietzsche's perspectivism, by contrast, there is rather "divergence," and each point of view is like another city linked to the others through differences, such that there is "always another city in the city." Similarly, unlike Leibniz's "windowless" monads, Whitehead's "prehensions" would, as it were, be all window; in PLI, Deleuze compares the monad to the minimalist vision of a car speeding down a highway at night with only its headlights to illuminate its view on the world.

37. DR, pp. 126ff. See QP, pp. 71–73, where Deleuze says our problem today is to invent a new persona for an "empiricist conversion" to again restore our belief in the world.

38. In CC, pp. 111ff, Deleuze says that problem pragmatism poses as to what human community must be for truth to be possible is at bottom a question of truth and trust. The pragmatist theme of *"confiance"* (trust, confidence) in William James in elaborated by David Lapoujade, op. cit.

39. On the figure of the "forger" in Nietzsche, Melville, and Welles in those situations where one must believe without being able to first determine what is true or false, real or unreal, see C2, pp. 173ff. On the role of such "forgery" among the *dramatis personae* of Zarathustra and its relation to nihilism, see "Nietzsche" in PI.

40. DR, p. 122.

Chapter 5

1. MP, p. 13.

2. MP, pp. 95ff.

3. For Deleuze, what Spinoza called "common notions" are not to be confused with abstract universals; rather they are "practical ideas," which turn his *Ethics* into a kind of experimental art of living.

4. Antonio Negri elaborates the notion of "multitude" in Spinoza along such lines in *Savage Anomaly: Power of Spinoza's Metaphysics and Politics,* trans. M. Hardt (Minnesota, 1991).

5. Deleuze counts Gabriel Tarde as the inventor of "microsociology" (DR, p. 104, note 1); the notion of "micro" supposes a notion of "mass" (or "multitude") prior to class (see MP, pp. 267ff), requiring a logic more Leibnizian than dialectical or Hegelo-Marxist—as also in the case of Foucault's talk of "micropolitics" or, later, of processes of "subjectivization." On Canetti's distinction between "packs" and "crowds," notably in the movement of "masses" in cities, see MP, pp. 46ff. More generally, for Deleuze a society is defined not by its class contradictions, but by the "lines of flight" that expose the potential of "masses" not yet divided up as distinct classes—such as the lines of subjectivization of the urban "proletariat" of the last century and the problematizations they introduced.

6. D, pp. 125–126. This section is reintroduced in modified form in MP, pp. 254ff. The problem of "another time" in politics is a matter of potential or possibility; see François Zourabichvili, "Deleuze et le possible (de l'involontarisme en politique)" in *Gilles Deleuze: une vie philosophique* (Institut Synthélabo [PUF], 1998), pp. 335ff—a matter of diagram and diagnosis of the "individuation" of new forces. In this sense politics becomes a matter of experimentation with that for which there preexists no theory, no science.

7. C2, pp. 281ff.

8. K, pp. 29ff.

9. On relations of city and state, see MP, pp. 539ff; they in turn are related to the question of violence in MP, pp. 558ff.

10. On the lack of "sufficiently deterritorialized cities" in formation of a modern German philosophy, see QP, p. 99.

11. MP, p. 32.

12. See "Immanence: a life" in PI.

13. Etienne Balibar credits Locke rather than Descartes with the "invention of consciousness" (John Locke, *Identité et différence*, introduction by Etienne Balibar, Seuil, Paris, 1998). Deleuze's "unconscious" might be then understood in contrast with the Lockean person or self, along the lines in which, for example, the "time-images" in cinema depart from conscious memory and empirical succession of a person or agent, and introduce another "impersonal" play into the notion of "characters." Rorty also proposes to view pragmatism in contrast with the classical "veil of ideas," yet without arriving at the sort of "impersonal unconscious" that Deleuze conceives in his "pragmatism of multiplicities."

14. Deleuze develops a concept of *autrui* as "expression of a possible world" in contrast with Sartre, who still worked with problems of subject, object, and futile "recognition." See LS, p. 360, note 11. That this concept goes beyond what Leibniz (and modal logicians) think of as a possible world as well as Wittgenstein's view of the expression of pain, see QP, pp. 22ff.

15. PP, pp. 165ff.

16. On the importance of Bichat in Foucault's thought, see PP, p. 150; Foucault's discussion of finding a "singular style" of dying makes Bichat a source for both Freud and Heidegger. See *The Birth of the Clinic* (Tavistock, 1973), pp. 140ff.

17. On the problems of singularity and impersonality of death, see LS, pp. 177ff and DR, pp. 148ff.

18. "Immanence: a life" in PI.

19. Michel Foucault, *The Use of Pleasure*, p. 11.

20. See, e.g., DR, pp. 374–376. The problem of "simulacrum" in DR (cf. LS, pp. 292ff) is not to be confused with Bau-

drillard's "postmodern" use of the term; in particular, it supposes a different relation to the "everyday" not based in theory of alienation, which runs throughout Deleuze's writings (shown in his emphasis on small differences rather than identities in Warhol's series). We see it not simply in the concept of Dadaist "machines" (with their uncoupling from recurrences); it is also found in the discussion of cinema. The question of "ceremonies of waiting" in Warhol's cinema (C2, pp. 249ff), for example, belongs to a larger discussion not simply of "gestus" but also of cinema itself as a kind of "automaton" (see C2, pp. 342ff). If obsession is the "pathology" of mechanical repetition (D, p. 371), perhaps "cognitive deficiencies" of the computer-brain have become those of the age of informational automata.

21. FB, pp. 60ff. The "problem of pure logic" that Deleuze thinks painting discovers through its own means—that of "the pictorial fact" (p. 102)—is tied up with this question of aesthetic chance or possibility. On the distinction between chance and probability, see N, pp. 29ff and DR, pp. 361ff.

22. MP, pp. 298ff. Deleuze admired Foucault's introduction to the lives of infamous men as small masterpiece: "It is the opposite of Georges Bataille: the infamous man is not defined by an excess in evil, but etymologically as the ordinary man. . . . To be an infamous man, was something like a dream of Foucault, his comic dream, his laugh to himself. . . ." PP, pp. 146–148.

23. CC, p. 13; on the relation of such "indefiniteness" to the "becoming-child" of philosophy in Spinoza, see MP, pp. 313ff.

24. LS, pp. 138–142.

25. DR, pp. 132ff.

26. See Michel Foucault, "The Confessions of the Flesh" in *Power/Knowledge,* ed. Colin Gordon, Pantheon, 1980, pp.

219–220: "The real strength of the women's liberation movement is not that of having laid claim to the specificity of their sexuality and the rights pertaining to it, but that they have actually departed from the discourse conducted within the apparatuses of sexuality."

27. CC, pp. 100ff. The problem becomes how to relate to one another by "feature, zone, function" rather than through identification with a prior model or law.

28. Cf. QP, pp. 104–105: "Heidegger was mistaken about people, earth, blood," since those who think are in fact never "majoritarian," never "landed" anywhere.

29. MP, pp. 437ff.

30. SSP, pp. 125ff. In PP, pp. 137–138, Deleuze reads Foucault's distinction between moral codes and ethics concerned with "styles of life" in this Spinozistic way, rather than through the Hegelian distinction between *Sittlichkeit* and *Moralität*. The first consists in obligatory rules to judge actions or intentions according to transcendent values, whereas the second is a set of rules one is free to adopt to "evaluate what we do, what we say according to the mode of existence that it implies."

31. K, pp. 131ff. Deleuze suggests constructivism might be seen from this angle (p. 136); see his remarks on politics and architecture, PP, p. 215.

32. For Deleuze, Plato's chora poses the problem of "the immanence of the Earth" (CC p. 171); he takes up the question in relation to Whitehead's reading of the *Timaeus* in PLI.

33. I discuss Nietzsche's idea of an Earth become light in my *Constructions*. The problem of Earth and territory in music or dance might be applied to Black American music (in its relation to Black English as "minor language"), from the classical urban forms of jazz to contemporary electronica and DJ mixes.

34. MP, pp. 381ff. The translation of *ritournelle* by "refrain" strikes me as somewhat unfortunate, since a *ritournelle* is just the opposite of a *rengaine.*

35. "Intellectuals and Power" in Michel Foucault, *Counter-memory, Language, Practice* (Cornel, 1974), p. 104.

36. MP, pp. 2533ff, distinguishes different kinds of seg-mentarities, all of which may be seen in Fernand Léger's 1919 painting, "Men in the City." But as one passes from such "me-chanical" divisions to the more sinuous or continuous ones Deleuze describes in "Societies of Control," there arise new dangers, which recall the warning with which the book ends (p. 625: "never believe that a smooth space will suffice to save us").

37. For Foucault, problems of urban demography supplied a key source of the problems that led to the formation of the disciplines. See "The Eye of Power" in *Power/Knowledge,* pp. 151–152. The two versions of the essay on the politics of health in the eighteenth century also establish a relation between hy-giene and normalization in cities.

38. PP, p. 234.

39. "Hume" in PI.

40. MP, pp. 539ff.

41. MP, p. 575.

42. *The Foucault Reader (ed. Paul Rabinow, Pantheon 1984),* p. 35. See my *Philosophical Events,* pp. 21ff.

43. See Michel Foucault, *"Il faut défendre la société"* (Seuil/Gallimar, 1997).

44. Michel Foucault, *The History of Sexuality, vol. 1* (Random House, 1978), p. 150.

45. On this point, see my *Truth and Eros* (Routledge, 1990).

46. Gilles Deleuze, "Désir et plaisir" in *Magazine littéraire,* no. 325, Oct. 1994, pp. 59ff.

47. PSM, pp. 71ff. See my *Truth and Eros* (Routledge, 1990).

48. CC, pp. 126ff. See also "Nietzsche" in PI.

49. CC, p. 42.

50. MP, pp. 235ff.

51. The "time out of joint" is a time "to come," yet not a messianic time; in Marx, it is instead a question of rethinking ideas of tragedy and farce in the eighteenth-century Brumaire. DR, pp. 123ff.

52. LS, pp. 77ff.

Chapter 6

1. CC, pp. 158 and 169. Deleuze thinks Spinoza is the one to pass beyond judgment notably in his critique of the "theologico-political."

2. CC, p. 17.

3. C1, p. 8.

4. CC, p. 169.

5. SPP, p. 128. Deleuze enlists Hölderlin and Kleist (rather than Goethe) to "understand" the differences between the two kinds or two senses of plan. Resonances of this kind, which help at once to elucidate art and philosophy, are to be found, for example, in Loos's remark upon meeting Wittgenstein—"you are I!"

6. C2, pp. 365ff.

7. C2, p. 219.

8. PP, pp. 192ff; and on Spinoza's style, see pp. 224–225.

9. QP, pp. 63ff.

10. On Warhol as a figure who continues Flaubert's image of attacking "stupidity," see Foucault, "Theatrum Philosophicum," p. 361, as well as the revised version of the essay on fantasia of the library.

11. C2, pp. 342ff.

12. QP, p. 187. In making the plan of composition "inform-ative" while making sensation depend on the "opinion" of the spectator concerning whether or not it is art, Deleuze thinks conceptual art risks missing both concept and art, as though it were unable to attain that zone of the unthought, prior to regu-larities that interconnect images and words, within which con-cept and art in fact encounter one another.

13. I discuss the problems of abstraction and diagram in my *Constructions* (MIT, 1998).

14. Foucault, "La folie, l'absence d'oeuvre" in *Dits et écrits* I, pp. 412ff.

15. "L'Epuisé," post-face to Samuel Beckett, Quad, 1992.

16. QP, p. 192.

17. FB, p. 56. In her *Sahara: l'esthétique de Gilles Deleuze* (Vrin, 1990), Mirielle Budens usefully works out the relation between the theme of Sahara and the discovery of an expressive materiality prior to "good form" (and so to matter or content); in a preface to this book Deleuze ties such "unformal" expressive materials to "what is essential for me, this 'vitalism' or concep-tion of life as non-organic power" (p. 6).

18. C2, p. 349. Deleuze makes an original use of the "other criterion" of the loss of verticality and frontal vision: as a distin-guishing feature of the "electronic image" (video and digital); see also PP, pp. 76–78.

19. C2, p. 33. In this respect, Deleuze's book not only de-parts from the "gaze-theory" inspired by Christian Metz, but also the "spectacle-theory," which sees image as "alienation" brought on by commodification. The problem of the image in neo-Realism (in contrast to the Marxist criticism of lack of "agency") for Deleuze forms part of an art of seeing something

intolerable in new situations for which there exist no means of description and judgment. The distance from spectacle-theory helps explain why Deleuze was never drawn to the category of the postmodern. The problem of creating a new kind of "image" is found at once in so-called modern and postmodern works.

20. Martin Heidegger, in *Poetry, Language, Thought* (Harper, 1971), pp. 79ff, says that *aisthesis* understood as "sensuous apprehension in the widest sense" or as *Erlebnis* is "the element in which art dies," over several centuries. For the "origin" of art would lie instead in unconcealing the world of a historical people or *Volk*. I discuss Deleuze's idea that in such passages Heidegger mistakes the ideas of both "people" and "Earth" in my *Constructions* (MIT, 1998).

21. DR, p. 94. See LS, p. 300.

22. DR, p. 79. Foucault makes this passage central to a review of this book; DE I, 767ff. On "transcendental empiricism" see "Immanence: a life" in PI.

23. Jean-François Lyotard, *Discours/figure* (Klincksieck, 1972).

24. MP, pp. 614ff. Drawing on Henri Maldiney, Deleuze proposes to see Riegl's distinction from the original angle of what he calls "smooth space"; one result is to rethink Pollock and abstraction, in a manner that continues the peculiar "Eygptianism" of Bacon. FB, pp. 79ff.

25. In a chapter in *Difference and Repetition* devoted to the "asymmetrical synthesis of the sensible," Deleuze distinguishes between extended space and an "intensive space" prior to it. *Effondement* (ungrounding) characterizes this intensive space of asymmetrical synthesis. See my *Constructions*.

26. MP, pp. 454ff. See my *Constructions*.

27. Henri Maldiney, *Regard, parole, espace* (L'âge d'homme, 1973 and 1994), pp. 254ff.

28. QP, pp. 168–169. The idea of "the flesh," at once "pious and sensuous, a mixture of sensuality and religion" (p. 169), is already to be found in both Heidegger and Husserl. Deleuze thinks Foucault's unfinished genealogy of flesh as object of confession might help bring out a distance from it; but in contrasting Bacon's "meat" to it, Deleuze is obliged to take issue with Bacon's own view of religion or Catholicism in his work.

29. Jacques Lacan, *Télévision* (Seuil, 1974), pp. 39–40. One might read this allusion to gay science in relation to the humorous assertion that it is only saints (those who *"décharite"*) who laugh (p. 28). In Lacan's own work, we find a distinctive humor in Deleuze's sense of the term: unlike the irony based on relations between negation and the Law, it is given through sense and nonsense, as though Lacan were pushing through his Catholicism to a gay science prior to the Law and its Order— rather in the manner in which Deleuze proposes to see Oedipus as a comical figure in LS, pp. 236ff.

30. Cinema 2, pp. 265ff.

31. Cinema 2, pp. 62ff. Deleuze wants to push the idea of "attention" beyond recognition or reidentification objects, indeed to the point where it would function as a kind of antidote to the "distraction" of recognition. One method is through a "logic of description different from Russell's" (note 3, pp. 63–64), which might be developed by, as it were, introducing the element of time into Elizabeth Anscombe's principle that all action is action "under a description": the past would then be intrinsically "indeterminate" (or "virtual") since it is always capable of falling under new sorts of description in the present, the series of which would remain open. A life of a character (agent

or person) could be said to be at once "vague" and "singular" in a sense given through an art of "indefinite description," which allows for such indetermination or virtuality.

32. PP, pp. 107ff. With television there is a loss of the world cinema had explored through its time-images; and for the "virtual public" of cinema one would substitute the more "sociological" one of television ratings and more generally a professional "control of the eye" enamored of information or communication and nothing else. But what then does it mean to still speak of "art," or "becoming-art" of these new forces? At the end of his letter to Serge Daney, Deleuze suggests that optimism may lie in a new global kind of "voyage"—where one leaves one discourse behind and adopts Proust's motto that the true dreamer is the one who goes out to verify something (p. 110).

33. Deleuze says we can't look into the brain to find new ways of thinking or new cerebral "paths" (*frayages*); on the contrary, science must "endeavor to discover what there could have been in the brain for one to set about thinking in one way or another." PP, p. 239.

34. PP, pp. 240ff. Thus we shouldn't believe that the new ideas of "flexibility" (in contrast to "top-down" organization) are there to save us; on the contrary, we must identify the new kinds of "control" (as well as the unexpected other possibilities) that they bring with them.

35. FB, pp. 13–14.

36. QP, p. 169; see note 17.

37. CC, pp. 110ff.

38. C2, pp. 222ff. Godard would explore the "worlds" of both Catholic and revolutionary faith, with which, from the start, cinema would develop a special relation. More generally, in Deleuze's "empiricism" we find a contrast between belief or

faith in the Revolution and a "becoming-revolutionary": it is precisely the nature of "belief in the future, of the future" (DR, p. 122) that changes—no longer a matter of either prediction or prophesy, it becomes a question of diagnosis and experimentation with the unknown knocking at the door.

39. DR, p. 233. On the contrast between Pascal and Nietzsche and the respective roles of probability and chance in the way the "game of thought" is played, see DR, pp. 361ff.

40. QP, p. 72.

41. QP, p. 72. Cf. PP, p. 239: "Belief in the world is what we lack most; we have completely lost the world; they have dispossessed us of it."

42. DR, pp. 96ff. In Hume there is synthesis of habit that allows one to infer from the present that past that caused it, and the future to which it is likely to lead. With Bergson and Freud, we then discover a second synthesis in which the past becomes indeterminate and "virtual," its nature and force endlessly shifting as the present falls under new sorts of description. The third synthesis is then one that makes the future rather than the indeterminate past or the habitual present the source of a complex repetition or free differentiation.

43. C2, pp. 165ff. Perhaps one might include the "paranoia" of what William Burroughs called "control" in this tradition. On this view of nihilism, see "Nietzsche" in PI.